How to Make Big Money
at Home
in Your Spare Time

How to Make Big Money

at Home

in Your Spare Time

By SCOTT WITT

PARKER PUBLISHING COMPANY, INC., West Nyack, N.Y.

LIBRARY OF CONGRESS
CATALOG CARD NUMBER: 71–150091

Third Printing . . . . . June 1975

PRINTED IN THE UNITED STATES OF AMERICA

You Can Earn Big Money at Home in Your Spare Time

The 185 plans presented in this book are based on the most successful home businesses being conducted today. They provide clear proof that the opportunities for making big money at home are greater than ever before. How big this money will be depends, naturally, on your personal desires, capabilities, and the dollar goals you set for yourself as big. But the opportunities are there, and this age of impersonal computers and automated mediocrity has left consumers literally begging for a personal imprint of care and quality in the products and services they buy.

You can fill that need now and at the same time provide yourself with substantial financial rewards!

TOP EARNINGS RIGHT FROM THE START

The step-by-step guidelines in this book make it easy to

—Select a home business tailor-made for you
—Launch your business with little or no capital
—Earn good money right away
—Multiply your profits for lifelong independence

Thousands of people have done it. Now their success will be the basis for your success. Every step you take will be one that has *already been proved* by people who at this moment are earning excellent incomes in their spare time at home.

Following the path they have laid out for you, benefiting from their hard-won experience merely at the turn of a page, you'll be surprised at how rapidly you can develop your business to the point where it brings the kind of large, steady income you want.

The exciting fortune-building information in this book was drawn from a study of thousands of at-home ventures. This included an examination of how each is operated, what its profit-making record is like, and how best it can be repeated by others—which, of course, means *you*. From this search came the 185 outstanding businesses outlined here. They offer convincing evidence that anyone with initiative can become well-to-do in his spare time at home.

SPARE TIME NOW . . . FULL TIME LATER?

Each of these enterprises requires only your spare time, and can be conducted that way for as long as you wish. But be forewarned: Many a person has been virtually forced by profits to quit his regular job! Part-time businesses at home can make so much money and show a potential of making so much more that sometimes it makes no sense to remain another man's employee.

This is one time when a quitter is actually a winner!

LEARN THE PROSPERITY SECRETS
OTHERS HAVE UNCOVERED

The business plans in these pages have brought unusual success to people from all walks of life . . . blue collar workers, executives, housewives, the retired, students, laborers, shut-ins, clerks . . . all of whom are living proof of the wonderful profits available to home-based entrepreneurs.

For example:

- A woman on the west coast invested $250 for some simple equipment that put her in a business from which she now grosses $27,000 per year.

- A couple embarked on a plan that still is so new that few others have yet latched onto it. Starting with only $300, they now take in that much, on the average, each week.

- A man, spotting a real need in his community, filled it. An investment of a few dollars now nets him $225 weekly.

• A New York State resident is reaping rewards as the owner of a business few people ever dream of. He works Saturdays and an hour or two one evening per week. The earnings have helped him to purchase a new home and send three children to college.

As you read about these people in greater detail later, you'll learn that most of them had no special training in the field they chose, and yet each succeeded in developing a big-paying enterprise!

HOW TO GET THE MOST OUT OF THIS BOOK

Consider Chapters 1 and 2 your "navigators" that will guide you on a direct and easy course toward your goal of a highly profitable at-home business. Here you'll find a wealth of success-secrets which serve as the foundation for the remainder of the book.

The plans themselves are included in various chapter-categories according to the type of business they represent. For instance, home office projects are in Chapter 3, while mail order plans are in Chapter 4.

In most chapters there are five basic plans containing detailed guidance, followed by a wide selection of related plans, presented more concisely. Since the strategy outlined in the *basic* plans is equally applicable to those that follow, it's not repeated. Read the entire chapter and you'll be well-prepared to launch any enterprise it contains.

In fact, you'll discover that a careful reading of *every chapter* is extremely helpful no matter which type of plan you ultimately decide upon. The profit-techniques outlined in one can very often be adapted for use with another.

Six months from now, when your business is well established, you should read the entire book again. You'll find new insights that can make your profits multiply at an even greater pace.

And now let's get started!

SCOTT WITT

Contents

How to Make Big Money
at Home
in Your Spare Time

1

How to Choose the Right Business for You

You are a born businessman.

Everyone is a born businessman.

Strong statements? Not at all. Given the ambition, there is not a person with average intelligence and fair health who cannot succeed in his own business. The secret is in finding the *right* business.

And that's what, together, we are about to do. We're going to find the right business for you to launch in your spare time at home—an enterprise that will pay handsomely in terms of both money and satisfaction.

WHY IS FINDING THE RIGHT BUSINESS SO IMPORTANT?

Not long ago, I received a letter from a man who had read an article of mine on the vast opportunities open to people seeking to earn extra cash at home.

"I'm 38 years old, married, and have three children," he said. "I certainly could use some of that spare-time money you speak about. Please recommend a business for me."

I'm afraid my reply didn't provide what he requested. My files contain rather thorough information on hundreds of successful home businesses, and it would have been easy to pick one of these and forward the information to him. But it would have done very little good.

Ninety-nine chances out of a hundred, it wouldn't have been the right business for *him*. His letter simply had not provided enough information on which to base an intelligent judgment.

Other than his age and family status, he hadn't told me anything about himself—his interests and hobbies, the type and size house he lives in, his community, the time he has available, how much (if any) money he wishes to invest, how much he would like to earn, and so much else that is important in determining the type of business he should enter.

What my correspondent apparently failed to realize is that you can't select a business merely on profit potential. It was Nicholas Murray Butler, for 44 years president of Columbia University, who said: "Businesses planned for service are apt to succeed; businesses planned for profit are apt to fail."

What you've got to do, then, is find the service that you—as an individual—are best equipped to provide. Although every plan contained here is a proven money-maker, not every plan is for *you*. There are many factors about you and your life that set you apart from every other person who reads this book.

By reviewing these factors now, you'll be prepared to recognize *your* business when you read about it later on.

Before we start, I want to exact a promise from you. In the pages of this book you have access to the best home businesses in my files—some of the most lucrative enterprises being conducted at home today. Just as I didn't "hand out" one of these plans to my recent correspondent before I could learn more about him, I hope you won't try to pick one without the benefit of learning more about your own business personality.

You're going to begin doing that right now.

YOUR MOST VALUABLE ATTRIBUTE

The prime factor of your business personality is enthusiasm. Nothing you put into an enterprise is worth more. And you can only impart enthusiasm when you enjoy what you're doing.

One of the most successful businessmen I know runs an enterprise about which, until a very few years ago, he knew absolutely nothing. One day he had suddenly found himself the owner of a large and expensive piece of equipment—collateral on a loan that had been defaulted. The question was: What to do with it?

He thought of selling it, but something held him back. Each time he looked at the machine, he became more fascinated. It was such a powerful piece of equipment, it could do the work of ten men. He read up on it, and his fascination increased.

Then he was struck with an idea. Why sell it? Why not sell what it could *do?*

What began as fascination soon turned to enthusiasm, and as he met with favorable response in selling the service this machine could provide, the enthusiasm brought success.

The machine was a backhoe. It's used to dig sewer trenches. Not a very inspiring business for you or me, perhaps, but this machine was the first piece of equipment in what has become one of the most profitable contracting firms in its region. All because of the owner's delight in mechanized earth-moving tools and what they can accomplish.

A business is a long-term affair. It's not like a job that you take this week and walk out of a month from now. You've got to have staying power. Enjoying your business—actually having fun with it— will give you all the staying power you need. This kind of enjoyment is the key to continued profits.

HOW TO SELECT A BUSINESS YOU'LL ENJOY ·

Being new to you, just about any home business will seem like fun when you first get it under way. But like a shipboard romance, that initial infatuation can fade rapidly once you get your feet on the ground. If you want you and your enterprise to be long-term mates, ignore the glitter and look for true compatibility.

A business plan that is right for you will probably flash one or more signals to which you should pay due heed. Here's what to look for:

Hobby-Related. If a plan matches one of your hobbies, three quarters of the battle has been won. You chose the hobby because it was pleasurable; extending it into a business is an almost certain guarantee that the enterprise will also be pleasurable.

Scores of hobbies that have become sources of excellent spare-time income are related in forthcoming chapters. For example, Elton Canzi, whom you will meet in Chapter 8, thought up a unique way to *share* his hobby with others—for pay. As you review the various plans, look for *your* hobby.

Job-Related. You'll know it's the kind of work you like to do if the plan's field of endeavor matches a present or former job that you have enjoyed. Some of the most profitable ventures were started by people whose introduction to the business occurred in private employment.

Brawn vs. Brain. Just about any line requires a combination of physical and intellectual effort, but generally there's a predominance of one over the other. You can have a long list of educational degrees but still prefer to work with your hands in your spare time. Conversely, I've known people who work during the day at physical labor only to conduct after-hours businesses in such fields as bookkeeping, mail order, and employment counseling. The important thing is to have the plan match *your* preference.

Work Pattern. Some people enjoy following an established routine in their businesses, while others would rather face new challenges every day. The former tend to be methodical in nature, and the latter more creative. Which are you—and does the plan fit?

People Involvement. Various plans have varying degrees of involvement with other people, ranging from the business in which you work alone to the one that has you constantly meeting the public.

A friend of mine who retired a few years ago from his job as a teller in a small town bank found himself missing two things. One was the income to which he'd been accustomed, and the other was his contact with the public.

He resolved both problems, though, by opening an antique shop in his home. He thoroughly enjoys meeting the people who visit his shop to browse and buy, and he has fun conversing with those he meets at the auctions where most of his own purchases are made. His new-found enjoyment is matched by his new-found income.

As you progress through the forthcoming chapters, you should have no difficulty in selecting a plan that closely matches your own desired level of people involvement.

The Picture Test. Finally, give each plan that appeals to you the "picture test." Picture yourself operating such an enterprise. Imagine that you are carrying out the various phases of the plan. Is the picture vivid? Can you see yourself doing it day in and day out—and enjoying it? For the moment, forget about remuneration. You're doing it for fun. Is it still appealing? Is it obviously more than a shipboard romance? If so, both you and the business score a passing mark for compatibility and you are ready to move on to the second criterion in the selection process.

CAPITALIZE ON YOUR PRESENT ABILITIES

You'll get more mileage from your career as a home-based entrepreneur if you can draw upon the skills you already have at your command.

Examine the major benefits derived from capitalizing on your present abilities:

1. *You can start your business without delay.* Little time is spent learning new procedures and techniques. You are well equipped to begin earning money right away.

2. *Your efforts are more productive.* You accomplish much more when doing what you know best. The more you accomplish, the more you earn.

3. *You can make more intelligent decisions.* Being well versed in your field of endeavor enables you to recognize the strategic moves that can enhance your profits.

4. *You understand the requirements and the opportunities.* Your goal is realistic and therefore achievable.

YOU are the most important element in your business. Put the best of yourself into it.

YOU DO HAVE THE ABILITIES

Every ability you have falls into one of two categories, the *innate* and the *acquired*. But what a wide range of proficiencies emanates from these two categories!

Your *innate* abilities—those you were born with—might better be termed talents. These talents are not evident at birth, of course, because an infant knows little more than how to breathe, cry, suckle, and carry out certain other bodily functions in profusion. But as he develops, the normal child may demonstrate a tendency to excel in specific fields. Two little girls of the same age might start taking piano lessons simultaneously, only to have one progress with far greater rapidity. The one who is less talented at the piano might be a better dancer, or mathematician, or public speaker.

Your *acquired* abilities came to you in many ways. They began with your home training, continued with your schooling, and developed further in your job experiences. Your outside interests, your hobbies, your day-to-day life have all contributed to the abilities you enjoy today.

The important facts to remember are that we all have certain talents that are above the norm, and we all have a multiplicity of abilities acquired over the years. These talents and abilities, when put to work in the proper combination, can reap tremendous dividends.

I'm not talking about attributes that stem from genius. Few of us are so endowed. Nor are most top echelon business leaders, for that matter. They've reached the top because they've been able to recognize how best to utilize the talents and abilities they do have. To put it another way: They know what they know, and they know how to use what they know. You can and should do the same.

RECOGNIZE YOUR BUSINESS-RELATED SKILLS

Many of us tend to underrate ourselves. You may not realize that you have the specialized abilities required for a highly profitable business at home. But you do—and by the end of this book you'll know what they are. How? By learning that hundreds of other persons have capitalized handsomely on the very abilities you have always taken for granted.

Each chapter will give you a new insight into these attributes and how they can best be employed.

Usually when someone tells me, "I'd like to conduct a business at home, but I'm afraid I just don't have the ability," I reach into my file and pull out a folder containing several success stories. While looking them over, the person invariably comes upon one that causes him to comment: "Why, this plan is easy! I could do this! I used to. . . ." And he tells of some experience, training, or talent that relates to it.

It's the kind of pleasant surprise I think *you* will encounter quite often in the course of this book

GAIN NEW OPPORTUNITIES WITH EASILY-ACQUIRED APTITUDES

As you become familiar with the various plans presented here, you may recognize an outstanding need in your community for a specialized service or product for which you don't have the required training. Don't cross off the opportunity. If you have a sincere interest in the type of work involved, you should give serious consideration to learning the skills. It could provide for greater remuneration, in the long run, than some other undertaking for which you are presently qualified, but for which there is a lesser need.

FIVE WAYS TO LEARN YOUR NEW TRADE

Why be shackled by needless limitations when it's so easy to open up new profit vistas? Check these five basic methods of obtaining new home business skills:

Independent Study. The public library and the book store provide a wealth of material for gaining knowledge in practically any field you choose. A great advantage of independent study with the aid of text or reference books is that you can learn at your own pace, allowing yourself ample time to practice as you learn.

Adult Education Courses. Most high schools and many colleges offer courses in various skills that can be put to practical use in home businesses. The registration fees are generally nominal, and you are assured of qualified teachers and approved methods of instruction.

Correspondence Courses. Hundreds of correspondence schools are providing uncounted persons with new profit-making abilities each year. Some institutions, such as International Correspondence Schools, offer training in scores of fields, while others specialize in one trade. Many of these schools advertise in the mechanics magazines. You can also check trade publications dealing with the particular field in which you are interested.

On-the-Job Training. This is a modification of the old apprenticeship system. What's more practical than taking a job with an established firm? It need not be for long—sometimes just a few months will provide the rudiments you need.

I have in mind the man who a few months ago did some picture-framing for me. He'd learned that type of work while being employed part-time in an art shop. He soon realized that he could make twice as much by doing the work on his own. It didn't take him long to prove it.

Franchises. There is an increasing number of franchises that can be operated from the home. Many require only modest investments. The advantage is that you are provided not only with training in the specific skills, but also with general guidance and support based on the franchisor's vast nation-wide experience. Another bonus is that you get to cash-in on the name and reputation of a large, well-known firm.

It's clear, then, that there is no need to be held back by a current lack of proficiency if you are convinced that the field offers extra potential for profit.

TAKE A RESOURCE INVENTORY

What resources will you be able to draw upon in launching and operating your business? No two businesses are alike in the requirements they will make of you in these four categories:
- Money
- Time
- Space
- Assistance

Your selection of an enterprise will be at least partially based on how well it matches what you have to offer in each category.

Let's examine them individually.

Money. Every business takes *some* money to start, ranging from a few dollars for incidental supplies up to hundreds and perhaps thousands of dollars for the elaborate equipment required in particularly ambitious undertakings. Fortunately, most home businesses are in the lower range. But if you should favor an enterprise with greater financial requirements than you are able to meet out-of-pocket, there are effective methods of obtaining the needed cash. We'll deal with them in the next chapter.

It may be that you already have on hand some of the equipment or supplies required for the venture you undertake. A car, woodworking tools, a sewing machine, a kitchen range, electronics equipment—

these are but a few of the items you may presently have that can be put to profitable use. This is like money in the pocket because it saves you from having to make a special investment.

Time. The requirements on your spare time vary widely from business to business. That's why you should determine beforehand just how much time you will be able to devote. Equally important is the *nature* of your spare time. Will it be during the day, or at night? Will it fall only on weekends? Will there be large blocks of available time, followed by periods when there will be little opportunity to devote to your pursuit? Know the answers to these questions before you begin studying the various plans outlined in later chapters. Then select an enterprise with time requirements in line with what you have to offer.

Space. No matter how small your living quarters, there's a home business that will fit. Even a furnished room is not disqualified! Naturally, the less space you have, the more selective you must be. But there are so many profit plans outlined in this book that you *can* be very selective indeed.

In making the selection, however, don't neglect to look ahead. Successful businesses grow, and growth can mean physical expansion. The space you have may now be fine for the business you pick—but does it allow for any expansion? How much? If your quarters are cramped, try to choose a field that won't make increasing space demands.

Assistance. While most home businesses can be operated by one person alone, some are designed for husband-and-wife operation—or even husband-and-wife-and-children. Before embarking on one of the latter categories, determine just how much support you have from your family. Their help can be a great asset, but if you have doubts as to its continuing availability, better stick to the loner type of enterprise.

YOUR PROFIT GOAL AS A GUIDE

Ask most people thinking about starting their own home business how much money they want to make and they'll reply: "As much as I can!"

Dreaming about making a lot of money has a purpose—it provides motivation. But dreaming alone will get you nowhere. You have to convert your dreams to practical application, and this requires a specific goal.

As explained earlier in this chapter, you won't choose your business merely on the basis of its profit potential. To do so could mean you'd select the wrong pursuit and there would be little or no profit at all. But certainly, profit will be *one* of the guiding factors in making your selection.

If your desire is to earn $25,000 or $50,000 per year, there is little point in picking a plan that shows promise of drawing no more than $5,000 or $10,000. On the other hand, if all you require is extra "pin money" of, say $50 per week, why become involved in an elaborate business plan that will take more of your time and energy than you need to devote?

In determining your profit goal, you should first analyze the basic money-desire that underlies your wish to embark on a part-time undertaking.

Is it to receive supplemental income regularly for many years?

Is it to raise a pre-determined amount of money by a certain time in order to achieve a specific purpose, such as buying a new home or educating a child?

Or is it to build a business which can eventually be converted to a full-time operation, allowing you to quit your present job?

These are three quite different goals, and there are few businesses in this book or anywhere that are equally capable of meeting all three. That's why it's necessary first to determine why you want to go into business . . . and then make your selection with this motive in mind.

As you read this book, check-mark the businesses that fit your goal. Later you can review and compare them on the basis of all the criteria outlined in this chapter.

YOUR BUSINESS MUST MEET THIS REQUIREMENT

If your business is to be successful, it must fill a need. The greater the need, the greater the success will be. No business that does *not* fill a need can be successful for very long. It's a basic rule, and it cannot be violated.

Throughout this book you will meet hundreds of people who have achieved a great deal of success in their home enterprises, and you can be sure that every one of these ventures does fill a need. But some of these same businesses could be operated in other communities by the same people and meet with failure. Why? Because the same needs do not exist in all communities.

Filling a need by no means confines you to providing the basics in life such as food, shelter, and clothing. The increasing affluence and the greater free time enjoyed by most people today have brought a corresponding increase in their "need" for second cars, extra television sets, summer homes, larger record and book collections, finer furnishings, club memberships . . . the list goes on and on.

So, in terms of business, a "need" can be defined as any product or service for which a sufficiently large proportion of the population is willing to pay.

HOW TO DETERMINE THE NEED FOR YOUR BUSINESS

In considering a particular type of business, there are three signs in your community to look for. Any one of them can indicate a significant need.

1. *A void.* There are no such firms in the community, but neighboring communities do have them and have demonstrated they are able to support them.

2. *A shortage.* Although one or more such firms are located in the community, the number in proportion to the population is less than the regional average.

3. *A growth pattern.* Currently, the community seems well supplied with the product or service, but the area is growing rapidly. It is obvious that the demand will increase along with the population.

If none of these signs is apparent, or if you wish to make a further check before proceeding, there are various steps you can take.

One is to conduct a survey. Do it over the telephone, through the mail, or in person. Contact a sampling of the type of people you hope to serve. Ask them whether *they* see a need for your business and, more importantly, if it is the type of thing they would patronize.

You might do some test advertising. Offer your product or service for sale to a small number of potential customers. Since this is only a test, you need not actually *have* the product or *perform* the service;

those who respond to your advertising can be told you are temporarily out of stock or presently unable to accept additional clients. If this seems misleading, you can reassure yourself with the knowledge that some of the largest firms employ similar testing procedures—and many would not dream of embarking on a new venture until after it has been thoroughly tested.

Carrying the testing procedure one step further, you can actually open up shop—but on a limited scale. Start small and feel your way until you have a firm indication of how great the need is. Let the venture guide its own growth.

FIVE YARDSTICKS TO GUIDE THE WAY

These are the essential points to remember in choosing your home business:

1. Select a plan that you'll enjoy.
2. Capitalize on your abilities.
3. Choose a plan that makes good use of your resources.
4. Be guided by your profit goal.
5. Determine that a definite need exists for your enterprise.

By following all five of these criteria, you'll know that the plan you choose is the right one for *you*. And you will have laid the groundwork preparing you for use of the success techniques revealed in the next chapter.

2

How to Get Your
Money-Maker Rolling

A few months from now—perhaps even a few weeks—your home business will be under way and you'll begin to draw income. The amount and continuity of that income depend to a large degree on how well you employ the strategy you are about to learn.

Each of the plans in this book has its own individual procedures, of course, but there are certain general techniques—some of them little known—that can give a giant boost to any enterprise.

YOU CAN START WITH LITTLE CAPITAL— OR NONE AT ALL

With all of the exciting opportunities available, it's surprising that more people are not starting their own businesses. Undoubtedly, one of the chief reasons is their fear that large investments are required. How little do these people know!

Using some of the methods that follow, you can build a thriving business with very little of your own cash, or, perhaps, no personal investment at all.

Right off the bat you have an advantage in the fact that you'll be operating from home, eliminating the burden of having to buy or rent a business location. That leaves these items to be paid for:

1. Products and/or materials
2. Equipment
3. Advertising

Now let's see how you can do this with as little cash of your own as possible.

HAVE OTHERS FINANCE YOUR PRODUCTS AND MATERIALS

There is no need to tie up a lot of capital in merchandise, or if you manufacture products, in the materials used in the manufacturing process. In fact, some businessmen rarely lay out *any* of their own cash for these purposes. They wisely utilize other people's money, freeing their own capital for use where it will bear more weight in developing the business.

One method is to obtain extended credit from your suppliers. In some cases, credit of up to 180 days can be arranged—meaning that you probably won't have to pay for the items until long after they have been sold. When the products or materials you need are offered by a number of suppliers, you'll find it pays to "comparison shop" among them for the best possible credit arrangement.

An alternative is to accept products from your suppliers on consignment. This means that you don't pay for an item until and unless it's sold. If, after a reasonable period, it does not sell, you merely return it to the supplier. You may have to do some searching to locate companies willing to make a consignment arrangement with someone just starting out, but it's well worth the effort.

Or, your *customers* can provide the financing by paying in advance for what they buy. This is often the procedure when the product is made to order, requires special installation, or is not available to your customers from any other local source.

You can also encourage cash with order by offering premium gifts or small discounts.

A business that is *based* on customer financing is drop ship mail order. This is the system in which the dealer carries no merchandise in stock; he forwards the customer's money (minus his own profit) to the factory or wholesale house, and *they* mail the goods directly to the customer—using a shipping label supplied by the dealer.

OBTAIN EQUIPMENT WITH LITTLE CASH OUTLAY

If your business requires special equipment that you don't presently own, there's no need to fork over any sizable amount of cash to obtain it. Most equipment manufacturers are geared to the time payment system. They know that businessmen want to hold out-of-pocket investments to a minimum, and they make the items available for a relatively small down payment. After that, monthly payments come, hopefully, from profits.

An arrangement that could prove more advantageous is the *leasing* of equipment. This, too, is a "pay as you go" setup, only the payments are tax deductible. Under many lease plans you also have the option of eventually owning the equipment, with title changing to your name after a pre-determined period of time.

HOW TO SAVE ON ADVERTISING

It's difficult, if not impossible, to arrange for advertising on the time payment plan. Most media have a firm rule requiring cash with order or, at best, shortly after the first of the following month. So you've either got to foot it yourself or obtain the money from one of the loan sources to be outlined later.

One way to *hold down* your advertising costs, however, is to take out contracts with the media you plan on using most. You can get lower rates by contracting to purchase a specified minimum amount of advertising within a given period of time. If, for some reason, you do not live up to the contract and purchase less than the agreed upon amount, there is no penalty other than that you are billed for the rate applicable to the amount actually purchased.

It would be worth your while to ascertain if there are broadcast stations or publications in your area that offer commission advertising. This is a system in which you pay a percentage of the sales price for each unit sold.

HOW AND WHERE TO OBTAIN LOANS

That old bromide about our roads becoming nearly empty if we were to remove all the unpaid-for cars is equally applicable to business. The streets of commerce would be nearly empty if the unfinanced businesses were to be removed.

Financing is the key to outstanding profit. By using other people's money wisely, you enjoy leverage that provides far greater investment power than you would have on your own.

Here are the sources most frequently called upon:

Family and Friends. This is the first place to look, because these are the people who are probably most sympathetic to your goals.

Banks. If you have a good credit rating and if you can convince the loan officer that the enterprise will be able to generate more than enough income to make repayment as scheduled, this may be the source of your needed cash.

Personal Finance Companies. It's easier to obtain money here than from a commercial bank, but there's a relatively low limit on what finance companies can loan to an individual. The interest rates will generally be higher, too. But if you need only a few hundred dollars or so and want to avoid preparing financial statements and going through other red-tape procedures, this is worth looking into.

Commercial Factors. If you've got collateral, such as equipment, inventory, or accounts receivable, you'll probably find a friendly factor with waiting cash. These operations range from the highly respectable down to outright loan sharkism, so be especially careful of whom you deal with and what you sign.

Small Business Administration. There are several ways in which Uncle Sam can help. The SBA provides assistance in obtaining private financing such as bank loans; if banks are willing to put up only part of the required cash, the SBA can lend the remainder. If no bank funds are available, the SBA is authorized to make direct government loans. Sixty field offices are located in key American cities. Contact the nearest.

Small Business Investment Companies. These lenders obtain their funds from the federal government and from private investors. They exist for the sole purpose of helping small enterprises get on their feet and grow. The local SBA office can provide you with a list of SBIC's covering your area.

TWO OTHER SOURCES OF CAPITAL

Don't overlook the possibilities of entering into a *partnership* or *franchising* agreement. A silent partner can provide your needed funds; you do the work, and you split the profits.

There's a growing number of national franchising companies offering business plans that can be operated from the home. All of them provide financing, some as much as 100%. You'll learn more about these in a later chapter.

FOUR VITAL ELEMENTS FOR SUCCESS

If you were to set out on a cross-country tour to examine hundreds of profitable at-home businesses, you'd discover that practically all of them have followed four basic rules to achieve their success. You'd see the same thing if you were to inspect the case histories in my files.

And, equally important, you'd note that most *un*successful home enterprises had failed to adhere to at least one of these rules.

1. Offer value, but be well paid.
2. Start small and grow with experience.
3. Control expenditures.
4. Use promotional techniques.

Now, briefly, let's take a closer look at each of these rules.

OFFER VALUE, BUT BE WELL PAID

There's no contradiction here. You *can* provide excellent value and at the same time achieve an enviable net profit. Working from your home spares you a large proportion of the overhead faced by many of your competitors. Pass part of the savings on to your customers. You'll still be ahead.

You can do this in one of two ways. One is to undersell your competitors while providing products or services of a quality that matches theirs; the other is to give an extra measure of quality—exceeding theirs—but at the same price. In other words, offer an "extra" in terms of either savings or quality.

Walter B. provides an example. His spare-time income-producing activity is printing, and he specializes in business cards. His equipment is in his basement, while all of the other printers in town occupy rented quarters. With the money Walter saves on rent, he's able to offer raised printing at the same price his competitors charge for standard work. You can guess who does most of the business card printing in *that* town.

START SMALL AND GROW WITH EXPERIENCE

When you've discovered a business plan that you are convinced is an excellent income opportunity, the temptation is to give it the double-barreled treatment to spur its full profit potential right from the start. Don't. Only experience in the actual operation of the venture can tell you which growth-avenues you should take.

To illustrate, a couple came to me asking for help in straightening out their mail order business. They had published an excellent booklet on floral arranging and had advertised it in a leading women's magazine. The ad brought response exceeding their expectations. On the basis of this, they immediately placed ads in nine other magazines, expecting the same degree of success.

It didn't work that way. The sales failed to pay even half of the advertising costs, let alone the cost of printing and mailing the booklets.

I explained to them that they had moved much too rapidly, and I helped them set up a careful program of testing various advertising media to determine which would bring profitable results on a continuing basis, and which should be dropped.

They followed that program and soon were advertising regularly in selected media. Using some of the techniques you'll learn in the chapter on mail order, their profits increased month after month.

What they did, in effect, was to start anew on a small scale, allowing the experience they gained with each step show them where the next step should be. There's a lesson in this for you, no matter what field of business you enter.

CONTROL EXPENDITURES

The first flush of success has encouraged too many budding businessmen to spend far too much on luxuries their firms don't need and can ill afford. A hefty gross profit is meaningless if your expenditures are so large that no net profit remains.

Buy the tools and supplies you need, certainly. But limit your spending to those items that have a direct effect on the advancement of your undertaking, and which will be able to pay for themselves through increased income.

USE PROMOTIONAL TECHNIQUES

First a definition: In the sense intended here, promotion involves any program, other than purchased advertising, designed to draw attention to your business and customers to your door. It's an effective means of supplementing a limited advertising budget, and it enables you to attract customers whom you might not be able to reach through normal advertising channels.

Regardless of the nature of your venture, there are scores of easy, inexpensive promotional techniques you can use.

Some examples from my files:

- The owner of a telephone answering service allows the use of his facilities during the annual charity "radiothon" on a local broadcasting station and thereby gets numerous free plugs on the air.

- The operator of a home-based beauty shop writes a weekly column on beauty for the local newspaper and has gained many new customers among those who follow the column.

- A kennel owner regularly inserts circulars under the windshield wipers of cars parked at dog shows in his region.

- The owner of a small village inn in an area popular with tourists is also a real estate broker, and he provides each of his guests with a mimeographed list of the available summer home sites. Many thousands of commission dollars have gone to the innkeeper-broker in this manner.

Throughout this book you'll find hundreds of strategic moves you can make to promote new business. Where they apply, use them!

DEVELOP THESE ADDITIONAL PROFIT SOURCES

Your customers will come to you to buy the specific products or services on which your business is based. But if you leave it at that, you'll be throwing away what can be a lucrative source of additional income.

In short, you should *diversify*. The object is to get your customers to buy, in addition to your regular product or service, *other* products or services.

You already know how a number of firms do this. Take a look at the corner drug store with its assemblage of products entirely un-related to the medical field. Or the ads you receive from *Reader's Digest* peddling record albums.

Usually, however, the products or services do have at least some relationship. Examples would include the insurance agent who sells mutual funds and the automatic car wash that sells car cushions and trash receptacles.

Diversification is easy in a home business because it usually in-volves no more than drawing a customer's attention to your sideline items when he makes his regular purchase from you.

If, for example, you ran a toy repair service in your home, you might *sell* toys as a sideline. They'd be on display in the room where customers drop off and pick up the toys brought in for repair.

Many of the business plans contained here have suggestions for diversification—but in most cases the opportunities are so clear that you'll have no difficulty in spotting them on your own.

WHEN AND HOW TO EXPAND

The day that you are pleased with your business—the smooth manner in which it is running, the money it's paying—is the day you should think about expanding. Sounds paradoxical, doesn't it? When you finally eliminate the bugs and develop a well-oiled machine, the time has come to create new problems and, in effect, start all over again!

The answer is that no good businessman is ever satisfied with the status quo. Business is dynamic, and the more involved you become the more dynamic you'll be, too.

Let's look at some of the ways a home business can be expanded.

Increasing the Output. This is the usual first expansion step, and the simplest. It involves increasing your capability to produce and sell your product or service. It is achieved by obtaining more production equipment and/or by hiring employees. It might also call for stepped-up advertising.

Those who lack space in their homes to accommodate a work force frequently farm out some of their work to others in the community. There's never a shortage of such help because people are constantly seeking ways to earn money at home.

Developing New Lines. This is similar to the diversification mentioned earlier, but on a broader scale. It involves more than offering incidental items that, although profitable, remain subordinate to the main product or service. This type of expansion calls for developing additional full-fledged lines to be sold through the channels you have developed for your initial endeavor. Examples: The mail order book dealer who adds correspondence courses; the stenographic service that adds a telephone answering service.

Wholesaling. Home businessmen who sell directly to retail customers can often find a greater market by convincing stores to handle their merchandise. Because the stores take over responsibility for the retail sales, more time is available for production to match the increased demand.

Franchising. Many an entrepreneur who has developed a unique product or service in his home has realized tremendous profits by selling regional rights to it in other parts of the country. The financial benefits can actually be twofold: The sale price of the franchise, and the continuing income from supplies sold by the franchisor to the franchisee. Some franchisors also charge monthly royalties.

Converting to Full Time. When a business has consistently paid a lot more, per hour, than your regular field of employment, the time has come to consider leaving your job to devote your full efforts to the enterprise. In fact, for many starting in their spare time at home, this is the ultimate goal.

Moving Out of the Home. Your success in building a business can eventually mean that it will outgrow your home, with that growth dictating a move to larger quarters. Although by this time you will probably be working full time at the venture, it's not a must. Employees can handle the hour-to-hour details—under your semi-absentee management.

MAKE YOUR EXTRA PROFITS WORK FOR YOU

Having read Chapter 1, you have set a profit goal for your enterprise. If you're the kind of businessman I think you'll be after activating the money-making forces in this book, you'll not only meet the goal, you will exceed it.

It's not too early to begin thinking about what you will do with those extra dollars—the profits over and above your spare-time income needs. It's tempting, I know, to spend them on luxuries you've denied yourself for far too long. A boat, a summer home, a trip to Europe—these are all highly desirable and could quite possibly be within your reach.

But if you avoid the temptation and put your "surplus" profits to work for you, your long range benefits can be far greater. Wise investment of this money in the growth of your enterprise will reap dividends that can put many more surplus dollars in your pocket in the future, and on a regular basis, too.

You might follow the example of Frank T., who established what he called a "growth fund" soon after his addressing service was launched. Frank put a percentage of his profits into this fund every week, and held the money for the day he could use it to expand his business.

He admitted to me that at first he didn't know just what that use would be. His hand-fed addressing machine had a sufficient capacity to handle all of the orders he was receiving in the early days of his business. But as he became known, more orders began coming in, and some of them were quite large.

When Frank recognized the need for a fully automatic machine, his growth fund was able to provide it for him. He can now handle twice the volume of business in the same amount of time. His profits have increased correspondingly.

TECHNICAL ASPECTS OF LAUNCHING YOUR BUSINESS

Before starting any home business, there are three vital questions to be answered.

1. What form will the business take—sole proprietorship, partnership, or corporation?

2. Should I take out insurance, and what kind?

3. What records will I have to keep?

We'll deal with these questions one by one.

CHOOSING THE FORM OF YOUR BUSINESS

Sole Proprietorship. Most home-operated companies take this form, at least initially. It's the simplest type of business organization you can create. Since you are the sole owner, you maintain single-handed control over the entire operation. There is relatively little governmental interference, there is no income tax on the business (just on you as the owner), and you enjoy the greatest amount of privacy available in any form of enterprise.

There are disadvantages to a sole proprietorship. You hold unlimited personal liability for your business debts, the line of credit is confined to your own individual credit rating, and the scope and growth of the enterprise are restricted by your own abilities and energies.

If a proprietorship is to be operated under any name other than your own, it should be registered with your county clerk. This will ascertain that you are not infringing on any existing trade name, and will help protect *you* from infringement in the future.

Partnership. This is almost as easy to form as a proprietorship, but has distinct advantages and drawbacks. On the plus side, it can create a stronger business organization, with the partners supplementing each other's contributions. One can provide the financing while the other contributes his efforts and abilities; or both can contribute equally in financing and effort to generate an operation much broader in scope than one alone could handle. Due to the combined ratings of the partners, greater credit may be available.

On the negative side, each partner has unlimited liability for the debts of the business—even those debts incurred by a partner without the knowledge and consent of the other principals. Partnerships are often subject to sharp disagreements, which can have adverse effects on the business. It can be extremely difficult to remove an unwanted partner. And the partnership automatically is terminated when any one partner withdraws, goes bankrupt, is declared insane, or dies. Thus there are potential complications to weigh carefully.

Corporation. Many businesses that begin as proprietorships or partnerships eventually become corporations. Few small home businesses are incorporated at the outset because of the expense and legal technicalities involved. But, depending on the nature of your business, there can be advantages. Your financial liability is normally limited to the amount of your stock investment in the corporation; your other personal resources are not endangered. It is generally easier to obtain new or additional capital. Ownership can be transferred more readily than in any other form of business.

Among the drawbacks is the initial cost of incorporating, which is usually a minimum of several hundred dollars, legal fees included. The firm is subject to greater governmental control, and also to an income tax; in addition to this, each stockholder is subject to individual taxation on whatever dividends or salaries he receives. It can be difficult to expand because of the burdensome legal requirements in doing business in states other than where the firm is registered.

INSURANCE

It's difficult to envision a business that does not need some form of insurance. Depending upon the nature and scope of your operation, you'll want to consider protection against: Damage to or loss of property; liability; personal injury; workmen's compensation; business interruption; death or disability of a partner.

The only way to determine what, if any, coverage you will need in each category is to confer with a competent insurance agent.

If you work alone at home, chances are that your needs will be minimal. Naturally, the more complex the operation, the more coverage you'll require.

RECORD-KEEPING

You *must* keep adequate records. In a home business, these don't have to be complex. If you are to conduct relatively few transactions per month, you can establish your own bookkeeping system, recording all expenditures and receipts as they occur. It will be to your advantage to open a checking account in the firm's name, using it solely for business-connected transactions. This way you'll have proof of your expenditures should they ever be questioned by an Internal Revenue agent.

Your local stationery store stocks simple forms and books that can assist you in establishing your record-keeping system.

Depending upon volume of business and frequency of transactions, you may wish to consult with a certified public accountant. He can set up a bookkeeping system that will be easy for you to maintain. Then, periodically, he will audit what you have done. You will thus be assured of having all data properly recorded, available for reference whenever required.

USE TAX ADVANTAGES TO INCREASE NET EARNINGS

As a home businessman, you will have a tax advantage enjoyed by few of your competitors. You can deduct from your income tax part of the expense of owning and maintaining your home *whether or not the cost of owning and maintaining your home is actually increased by the operation of your business.*

Let us imagine that your home has six rooms and that you have set aside one of these rooms exclusively for your business. Then the cost of heating, lighting, insuring, and maintaining that room can be legitimately deducted.

These expenses are not difficult to ascertain. What you do is determine the total expenses for your home and divide by six (since your "business room" comprises one-sixth of your home).

If you own your home, you are also entitled to take depreciation on that part which you use for business. If you rent, divide your rental by the proportion of your home or apartment that is used for business. (Again, if one room out of six is used for business, you would divide by six.)

Other business-related expenses you can deduct include:

Advertising	Repairs
Licenses and Regulatory Fees	Overnight Travel
Incidental Supplies & Materials	Heat, Light, & Power
Salaries & Wages (but not your own)	Bad Debts
Training	Entertainment
Dues to Business Associations	Insurance Premiums
Local Transportation	Interest on Indebtedness
	Business Taxes

To be fully familiar with *all* of the deduction and depreciation items, and how to deal with them on your tax return, send 75¢ to the Superintendent of Documents, Washington, D.C. 20402 and request the booklet *Tax Guide for Small Business*. Published annually, this publication answers in layman's language just about any federal tax question you may have.

By reading it, you will learn that you can deduct most items that are ordinary in your trade or business and necessary for its operation. The word "ordinary" refers to an expense which is a common and accepted practice in your field. The word "necessary" does not have to mean *indispensable*. It has been defined as a business expense which is appropriate and helpful in developing and maintaining the enterprise.

Many businessmen make the serious mistake of not taking full advantage of the deduction and depreciation items available to them. In fact, overpayment of taxes is listed as one of the major causes of business failure!

So read the *Tax Guide for Small Business* and become familiar with all of the tax savings available to you in your venture. If you still have questions, or if you need assistance, consult an accountant. His fee will likely be more than offset by the savings he can effectuate. Besides, the fee is deductible!

SHOULD YOU CONSULT AN ATTORNEY?

Depending on the business you choose, you may need to determine what, if any, local zoning regulations might affect your undertaking, what federal, state, or municipal laws govern its operation, and what health and safety requirements have to be met. Other legal considerations include the contracts you may have to sign, the wages you pay, the manner in which you handle your advertising, and even the nature of the product or service you sell.

Fortunately, most self-operated home businesses, being basically simple in structure and operation, face relatively few dictums from the governmental powers-that-be. But you do have to know what they are, and unless you have the time and know-how to check them out yourself, a lawyer is your best bet.

This is not to say that the responsibility should be placed in his hands alone. Economy requires that you do as much of the initial legwork as you can, leaving the thorny problems to the attorney—and then having him double-check what you've found out on your own.

In your first visit, be prepared with all of the basic information he'll need in order to provide the guidance you require. This will save needless effort on his part in ferreting out facts that you could have provided, and it will cut down on his fee.

True, there are firms that have gone on successfully year after year without ever once having called upon the services of an attorney. But they generally involve the most rudimental type of enterprise—and even so, they've been lucky. Counting on luck is contrary to all of the principles outlined in this book.

So, unless you're sure of the ground on which you and your business stand, seek legal advice. It will help provide the solid foundation from which will grow years of profit and accomplishment.

3

Carrying on a Profitable Home Office Project

You can start with as little as a telephone, a table, and a typewriter and you can grow as big as your inclination and vision allow. You can work with the knowledge that what you're doing is guaranteed to sell at a handsome profit—because it's been ordered in advance with the price-tag already attached.

Such are the reasons you should consider launching a home office project. It is one of the most fascinating, success-prone ventures on which you can embark.

MAKE BIG MONEY SERVING OTHER BUSINESSMEN

Service is the name of the game in home office projects. Your enterprise is geared to do for other businessmen and professionals what they don't have the time or facilities to do for themselves. Because you'll be helping them in their money-making pursuits, increasing their efficiency or profits, you'll be paid well. And thanks to low overhead, more of what you receive will be yours to keep.

HOW TO TRANSFORM ODD MOMENTS INTO A STEADY INCOME

The nine-to-five grind that many people associate with office work has no bearing here. Since your home will be your office, your hours will be whatever you choose.

They don't have to be "steady" hours. Many people—especially women with young children—do their home office work in bits and pieces, ten minutes here, half an hour there.

As one explained to me: "I can do the equivalent of at least four hours work each day by taking advantage of odd moments as they arise. It's surprising how rapidly these minutes add up to income-producing hours!"

So, take advantage of your spare moments. Find your diversion in making money instead of back-fence chitchat, turn on the desk lamp instead of the television set and you, too, will be pleased at the profitable hours you create.

Of course, everyone's time-finding system is different. I know a woman in the Midwest who performs her office assignments from midnight until eight in the morning. Why? Because her husband works that shift at a manufacturing plant. This way they enjoy more time together.

FIVE CARDINAL RULES FOR HOME OFFICE SUCCESS

Because your home makes for a somewhat unorthodox work environment, you'll have to take special steps to insure that you can function in a businesslike manner. It may be necessary to rule your work area off-limits to the youngsters, and you'll want to have a safe place in which to store your output. Although your home may not *look* like an office, it will be mandatory that you adhere to Rule Number One: *Establish businesslike surroundings for a fully professional output.*

Since you're working for another businessman, *his* standards and procedures must be complied with. That old maxim about the customer always being right fits perfectly here. Rule Number Two is: *Learn ahead of time just what is expected and then do everything possible to have that expectation met.*

A businessman who farms out office chores is in no less of a hurry than the one who maintains his own staff. He wants the work done by the time for which it has been promised. Rule Number Three: *Never make a completion-time promise that you cannot honor.*

The attorney who assigns work to you trusts that you will keep confidential the contents of the briefs and letters you type for him. The repairman for whom you prepare bills doesn't want the whole town to know his gross was down last month. The customer who uses your telephone answering service hopes that his messages are for his ears alone. Rule Number Four: *Your clients place a trust in you and it's your obligation to live up to it.*

The reason people send work to you is that it is more convenient than doing it themselves. Part of that convenience is the cost factor. The better your prices, the more work they will send your way. Rule Number Five, therefore, is: *Take advantage of your low overhead to undersell your competitors.*

AN EASY WAY TO EXPAND

Once you've adopted a plan in this chapter and your business is well established, you'll probably begin to think about expanding for an even greater income. A very effective way of doing this is to adopt a second plan from this chapter and add that service to your present enterprise.

The plans work well with each other. Tying in a second one can usually be done with ease. Because you've already established your clientele, there's a ready market for your additional services.

Plan 1: TYPING AND CLERICAL SERVICES

Fulfilling the typing and clerical needs of business and professional people in your community can be an interesting and rewarding enterprise.

Many women average $75 weekly and still manage to rear children, spend time with their husbands, and keep their homes in tiptop shape. Some do quite a bit better, using the business-expansion technique that will be explained.

Here are some of the services you can provide:

Typing. Material to be typed is delivered to your home. Sometimes it's presented to you in longhand, other times it's previously-typed material with some changes to be made.

Generally, the charge is 35¢ for each double-spaced 8½″ × 11″

page. Single-spaced pages are listed at 60¢. Lengthy manuscripts are typed at 65¢ per thousand words. With all work, a carbon copy is provided. Additional copies sell for 5¢ each.

Typing that does not fit in the above categories, such as legal briefs or the addressing of envelopes, is charged on an hourly basis. You might set your rate at either $2.50 or $3.00 per hour.

Dictation. The client calls you on the telephone and dictates letters, or sometimes the material has been dictated into a machine for you to transcribe.

With a standard goal of $2.50–$3.00 per hour, you can have two different arrangements. If a client has quite a bit of work at one time, you can charge a straight hourly fee. For those who have piecework, the charge is 75¢ per average letter page.

There's no need to rule out dictation merely because you don't know shorthand. A good cassette tape recorder can be obtained for about $50, it's very easy to use, and with it you can take and transcribe every bit of dictation you receive.

A simple gadget available in most electronics stores enables you to record telephone conversations on these machines. So, when your clients call in their dictation, you merely flip a switch and the material is all there on tape waiting for when you get around to it.

Billing. Most service businesses and all professional people send out monthly bills. You can handle this task for them and receive good pay for doing it. Since each job is different, you charge your hourly rate.

HOW TO BUILD YOUR BUSINESS

Go through the Yellow Pages in your telephone book and pick out the names of all doctors, attorneys, small service firms, and perhaps some retail merchants. Send each a carefully typed letter under a professional-appearing letterhead. Outline your services, explaining that they are available at modest cost. (But don't actually list prices; save this until you learn the specific needs of each prospect.) And insert an ad in the Yellow Pages yourself.

You can also run an inexpensive ad aimed at reaching writers who frequently need typing done for them. This ad should go in any of three magazines: *Writer's Digest, The Writer,* or *Saturday Review.*

They are available on most newsstands, and you'll see other ads on which to base yours.

TRY THESE EXPANSION POSSIBILITIES

As your client list grows, you may find that you're unable personally to handle all of the work offered. This is when you should think about farming out some of the tasks. Many *other* women are looking for spare time work they can do in their homes, and you will have no difficulty in getting them to do typing and take dictation for about $1.75 per hour. Since what *you* charge is on the basis of $2.50 or $3.00 per hour, this gives you a substantial profit on the work performed by your helpers.

In fact, you can eventually turn most or all of your work over to these at-home assistants and draw a good income by pocketing the difference between what you are paid and what you pay them.

Plan 2: TELEPHONE WEATHER REPORTS

Your telephone can be the source of regular spare-time income in a new profit plan that is just now becoming popular in a number of locations.

Fortunately for you, there are disadvantages to the methods by which most people obtain weather forecasts. Those printed in newspapers are at least several hours old and have frequently been superceded by more up-to-date forecasts. Getting the weather on radio or TV involves tuning in at a specific time that often is inconvenient, or else tuning in at random and having to wait until the forecast is given. Calling the special telephone company number costs money.

Here's how you can capitalize on the situation: Residents of your area will telephone a number you have set aside so that they may hear a recorded announcement containing the latest forecast. It will involve no expense to them and it will be profitable to you.

WHERE YOUR PROFIT COMES FROM

You are probably familiar with telephone answering devices that function when the subscriber is away from his phone. Every time the phone rings they give forth with a pre-recorded message—in this case, the weather forecast. And along with the forecast there will be a spoken advertisement on behalf of a local business firm, paid for by the firm. That's the source of your income.

Whenever someone calls your weather-number, he'll be greeted first by a 30-second commercial on behalf of the advertiser; in order to hear the weather he must listen to the message.

Sponsors usually "buy" the weather in three-hour segments. For example, the local bank might pay you for including its message during the 6 A.M. to 9 A.M. time period; another sponsor would be heard from 9 to noon, etc. You base your rates on the average number of calls received during a given time period.

HOW TO GET STARTED

First, rent a business telephone line and either buy or lease an answering device. Many electronics catalogs sell them for under $200, or you can lease one for a monthly fee. Check the Yellow Pages.

Second, make arrangements with the nearest U.S. Weather Bureau to obtain the forecasts as they are issued. If the nearest bureau is so distant that making a call to it four times daily would be prohibitive, you can obtain the forecasts by dialing the special telephone company number.

Third, announce your new service to the public in a conspicuous manner so that as many people as possible will know about "the free weather number." Insert ads in the newspaper on several different occasions, stressing the fact that there is no charge and that the forecasts are the official ones "compiled by the U.S. Government."

HOW TO OBTAIN SPONSORS

Until you receive a sufficient number of calls to make the service salable, you can insert your own message prior to the weather. Callers might hear something like this:

"Here's the latest weather forecast for Pleasantville and vicinity, brought to you as a public service by the Pleasantville Weatherphone Company. But first, an important message for businessmen. Here is a new and different advertising medium for reaching the many people who call this number for the weather. At a moderate cost, your advertisement can be included along with the forecast. You'll be providing a genuine service to the public and at the same time drawing many new customers to your place of business. For further details, simply call 247-8340. No obligation on your part, of course—and it may be the smartest business move you ever made! That number again is 247-8340."

The number prospective *advertisers* are asked to call can be your regular home phone number. Thus, the business line you've rented is used solely for the recorded forecasts, and your own personal line for conducting business.

You can, of course, speed up the process of obtaining sponsors by notifying them directly of your service by mail, phone, or in person. Set your initial rates low and raise them as the number of weather calls warrants. Your best prospects are businesses that tie-in with the weather, such as auto tire shops, rainwear stores, taxi and bus companies, etc. Special messages can be prepared for use when rain, snow, or other types of poor weather are predicted.

HOW TO EXPAND

As your enterprise becomes more popular, your callers will more frequently be encountering busy signals. When you've reached this stage your rates will be sufficient to finance the renting of one or more additional phone lines and obtaining more answering equipment.

A husband and wife who have achieved considerable success with the weatherphone business have expanded their service beyond the weather. Mr. and Mrs. Paul Kasten now set aside a number on which the inning-by-inning scores can be reported whenever their local high school plays an out-of-town game. On Election Night, they offer local returns.

The Kastens began their enterprise with an investment of about $300. It now brings in $300 per week on the average.

If this is the type of money-making plan that appeals to you, now is the time to go at it—before others in your community recognize how profitable it can be.

Plan 3: TELEPHONE ANSWERING SERVICE

One of the most successful at-home enterprises being conducted today is the telephone answering service. You can launch one practically anywhere—from a small town to a large city. Your investment can be minimal and you need no prior experience.

This business can take either of two basic forms—a message relay service started with just your own telephone, or a full-fledged answering system with the installation of special telephone company equipment.

Message Relay Service. Under this arrangement, you allow business and professional people to list your telephone as their own. The client periodically calls in to receive his messages.

Full-Fledged Answering System. When a client leaves his office, he throws a switch that will automatically relay all of his incoming calls to a switchboard installed in your home. When he returns, he throws the switch again and the connection between his office and your switchboard is broken.

HOW TO GET STARTED

The first step is to determine the need. How many answering services now operate in your community? (The Yellow Pages can answer this question.) Are the firms serving your community actually located *in* the community? (If they operate from another town, you can probably offer cheaper service because *you* won't have to rent long connecting lines.) Is there a sufficient number of potential clients to warrant your going into business?

Once you've determined that a need does exist, you must decide which of the two forms your business will take. The message relay service offers the considerable advantage of requiring a low investment. No additional telephone equipment will be needed at first, and your only expense of any consequence will be for promotion. With the more elaborate full-fledged system, you'll be leasing equipment from the phone company, but you'll be able to offer a broader range of services.

If you've decided on starting with "the works," a visit to the local telephone business office is in order to arrange for installation of a small switchboard. The phone company provides this on a rental basis.

Next, work out a plan for providing your answering service for as many hours as possible. While many businesses require their phones to be answered for only eight or ten hours per day, doctors and other professional people might desire round-the-clock service. The more hours you are able to operate, the more customers you can expect.

ADDITIONAL INCOME SOURCES

Although the decision need not be made at the outset, there are many other types of service that you can add, providing welcome sources of additional revenue. If you have a switchboard, you'll be able to transfer calls from a client's office to wherever he happens to be at present. Other services include wake-up and reminder calls, in which a client is phoned at a prescribed time, and mail relay, in which your home is used as the client's mailing address.

HOW MUCH TO CHARGE

Rates vary according to location, and you should first check what competing firms are charging. You'll probably find that straight phone service (in which the client's calls are re-directed to your phone or switchboard) sells for between $15 and $25 per month, plus whatever the phone company charges for a connection between the client's phone and yours, if there is a connection. Fifteen cents might be added for each toll-free transfer call. Mail could be collected for a nickel apiece, and reminder calls made for 15¢ each.

HOW TO BUILD YOUR BUSINESS

The best means of obtaining clients is, naturally enough, by advertising in the Yellow Pages. That's usually the first place someone seeking such a service looks. But since the next phone book might not be published for as long as a year, you may need to use other advertising media to get started. The business service section of your local newspaper's classified ad columns should prove profitable. An inexpensive circular or form letter can be prepared and distributed to likely prospects. These would include every doctor and dentist in the area and all service firms that handle off-premises work.

HOW MUCH CAN YOU EARN?

The amount of income that can be generated by a telephone answering service has been demonstrated by a couple I know, Mr. and Mrs. Peter Longo. They began several years ago with an investment of $250, starting with a message relay service. Within a few months it became apparent that with the addition of a switchboard their number of clients would rapidly multiply. It did—and now they have a total of four switchboards and two full-time women employees.

The firm has about 200 clients paying an average of $15 monthly. This accounts for an annual gross of $36,000. Roughly half of this is clear profit.

Plan 4: REPRODUCTION SERVICE

Most business firms have at least occasional need for reproduction of the various forms, documents, and papers they use—sometimes a few copies, frequently in large quantity. Many of them don't have the equipment to do this and must call on outside firms to handle it for them.

A home-based reproduction service can offer any, or all, of these reproduction methods:

- Photocopies
- Spirit Duplicating
- Mimeographing
- Photo Offset Work

Mr. and Mrs. Carl Douglas operate such an enterprise from their home in New York State. Mr. Douglas is disabled and thus cannot hold a regular job. He is, however, able to assist his wife in many of the functions of the reproduction service, which employs the first three of the above methods. The Douglases also handle photo offset work, but it is farmed out to a printer. Their income range is $8,000–$10,000 per year.

You can pick up the needed equipment at surprisingly low cost in relation to the income it is capable of producing.

Photocopiers sell for as little as $30 and go up into the thousands. For your purposes, however, a machine in the $200–$300 range should be best. Because many models have delicate mechanisms, it's best to buy one new.

Spirit duplicators can be bought for between $150 and $200 new, but you may be able to purchase a good used one in an office supply store.

Mimeograph machines can also be bought second-hand. You'll want an electric model, which can be obtained used for about $125 and new for anything between $150 and $300, depending on the brand.

Photo offset machines cost more and take a little more knack to operate. Rebuilt models that will handle most office needs are available for $600 and up. With these, it's usually best to arrange for a service contract once the guarantee has run out.

HOW TO OBTAIN CUSTOMERS

Elaborate advertising is not needed and, in fact, is not desirable in a reproduction service because you'll want to keep your prices competitive, and this involves a rather close profit margin. The old standby of the Yellow Pages is, of course, a must, and perhaps a small classified ad inserted regularly in a local newspaper would be warranted.

Many such firms get permission to install posters in stationery stores in their area, and some reproduction services make arrangements with stationers to serve as "drop points." The stationer takes the order and relays it to the repro service. Then, when the work is completed, the customer picks it up at the stationery store and pays the stationer, who deducts a small commission before turning the money over to the repro firm.

HOW MUCH TO CHARGE

The basic charge for photo copies should probably be 15¢ for the first copy of a given document, with a somewhat lower price—perhaps 12¢—for each additional copy.

Spirit duplicating is, of necessity, low volume work. Five hundred copies is usually the limit, and a penny a copy the price, with a minimum order of $2.00.

Mimeographing is practical for up to about 10,000 copies. Once again, the price should be in the neighborhood of $1.00 per hundred, but with a mimimum order of $3.00 to pay for the slightly more time-consuming procedure of attaching the stencil and getting the ink supply going.

If you go into photo offset work (and perhaps it's best to wait until you see how great the call is) you'll be able to demand a minimum order of $10, which pays for a thousand copies. From there, your rates go down as the quantity goes up. Admittedly, there are firms in some of the larger cities that handle the work for less—but they manage it by lumping jobs together on "gang runs" and their attention to quality is not as great as yours will be. In any event, it's generally more convenient for the customer to deal with you.

These prices are based on work being ready for reproduction. If you must prepare a spirit master, cut a stencil, or paste-up copy for photo offset, you'll charge for this added work on an hourly scale.

AN IMPORTANT THING TO REMEMBER

Buy your paper in quantity. You'll find that ten reams cost considerably less per sheet than by the single ream. A savings of 15–20% can spell the difference between a profitable business and a *very* profitable business!

Plan 5: ADDRESSING
AND MAILING LIST SERVICES

The increased competition for the shopper's dollar has caused a great number of business firms to increase their use of direct mail. You can capitalize on this trend by (1) renting them mailing lists of all heads-of-household in a given area, and (2) by maintaining the firms' own lists. Here's how it works:

Names for heads-of-household lists are obtained from the phone book or from the voter registration rolls. Each name is typed on a master unit and filed by community or section of community. You'll then be able to offer any businessman a complete list of names for the area your service covers, or partial lists based on whatever section or community he desires.

In the second type of service—maintenance of customers' own lists—the client turns over to you the names of people he has dealt with in the past and wants to reach again with notices of sales or other special events. *He* obtains the names from his invoices or monthly billing.

HOW TO BEGIN

You'll get started by deciding on the type of addressing equipment to buy. For this type of service there are three basic categories you'll want to consider.

Addressograph. This is probably the most common form of addressing used by small and medium-sized firms today. The names and addresses are embossed on metal plates, which are practically indestructible. This is important because you'll be renting the same names repeatedly. The drawback is the higher initial cost for equipment and plates. Rebuilt Addressographs sell for $800 and up. Plates go for 10¢–12¢ each.

Elliott. Lower initial cost and a lower cost per name and address are available here. This system uses little stencils that can be prepared on a regular typewriter. Each costs only a few cents and can be used for many hundreds of impressions. A relative of mine who operates a home-based business bought a used Elliott machine about ten years ago and reports the original machine and many of the first stencils are still in use.

Spirit System. This employs the same method as spirit duplicators. By typing on a special master card, you leave a coating of purple carbon. When you run the card through the machine, some of that carbon is transferred to the envelope by means of a solvent. The advantage is the ease and low cost of preparing and storing the masters. The disadvantage is their relatively short life.

Your best move would be to visit a number of office supply houses, determine what machines are available new and used, discuss their operating features with the salesmen, and choose a machine on the bases of cost and adaptability to your particular needs.

HOW TO SET YOUR PRICES

The usual charge for renting your own list (and this includes the labor involved in addressing) is $20 per thousand names. When maintaining customers' own lists, you'll charge according to a set schedule. This will include a charge for preparing each master unit based on your cost and time, and an addressing fee based on the speed with which your particular machine can function.

HOW TO OBTAIN CUSTOMERS

Make note of the firms that frequently mail out advertising pieces to "Occupant" or "Boxholder." Contact some of these companies and let them know of the advantages and low cost of having their mailings done on a "personalized" basis. Explain that recipients pay more attention to mail addressed by name.

Then you might contact small stores—especially those with merchandise selling for $50 and up. This type of merchant rarely can get by on "walk-in" customers. He depends on specialized advertising methods, and your regionalized lists should be a boon to him.

Naturally, you'll be listed in the Yellow Pages.

HOW TO EXPAND

Initially, you would probably do best to have a list no larger than 15,000 names. This is large enough to be profitable but not so large that it will be cumbersome while you're gaining experience.

Later you can expand by broadening the area you cover. The experience you will have gained in the initial stages will guide you in determining the time for, and range of, such an expansion.

The high profitability of this type of business is evident when you realize that each time you rent a 15,000 name list you receive $300. Rent it just once a week and you've got a spare time income that's hard to beat.

NINE MORE HOME OFFICE PROJECTS

Bookkeeping Service. Many small businessmen can't afford to hire a full-time bookkeeper and most don't have the time, inclination, or ability to handle it themselves. If you have a good background in bookkeeping techniques, you can work up a profitable enterprise providing this service for a few dollars per week to each client. Obtain your customers by sending out form letters to likely prospects (including all doctors and dentists in your area) and by advertising in the classifieds. As your business grows, you can add part or full-time help and expand as much as you wish.

Remail Service. For various reasons, people sometimes desire to have a letter mailed from a city or section of the country other than their own. Yours is not to question why—but to oblige them, and profit from it. Check the "personal" classified ads in any of the mechanics magazines and you'll see that a number of people are providing this service for about 25¢ per piece or $3.00 on a monthly basis. You won't get rich, but it can be a good source of added income.

Research Specialist. Writers often require specialized information involving time in the library; so do businessmen. Provided you have the time, you can earn a fair-sized and steady income by handling this task for them. Advertise in the writers' and literary magazines. Circulate business cards. Ask your friends to pass the word. Frequently, you'll find that one customer refers several others to you.

Proofreading. If you can give attention to detail—if you're the type of person who takes pleasure at catching misprints—this could be your money-maker. Look up all the publishers in your area or the nearest big city, advertise in the writers' publications, and you should find yourself with plenty of profitable reading to do.

Care-Ring. That's what a New York woman calls the service in which, for $17.50 per month, she telephones invalids and oldsters who live alone. She calls them twice each day at the times they choose—just to check that everything is all right. If there's no answer, another call is placed 30 minutes later. If still no answer, the service dispatches a registered nurse to the client's home. Obtain 30 clients and you have $575 per month.

Counseling Service. Got a special field of knowledge? Then you can be a personal or business counselor. A more interesting specialty would be hard to find. You can help soon-to-be brides, families with problems, slipping businesses, and individuals who seek to "talk out" their troubles. The pay is tops.

Ghost Writing. Many prominent people are called on to give speeches or write articles for business or organizational journals without having the first idea of how to go about saying what they *want* to say. This is why your flair for words can put a bulge in your wallet. You can't very well advertise yourself as a "ghost writer," but you can let it be known that you do speech and article preparation, euphemistically stating that it's a great "time-saver" for busy people.

Public Relations. Businesses, politicians, and some civic organizations are constantly seeking to keep their names before the public. If you've got the knack of preparing news releases and dreaming up attention-getting activities, you're in business. Do some publication advertising and send out notices to likely prospects and you'll be on your way. In this business, success with one client will soon have others at your door, so once you're established you should have little trouble growing.

Income Tax Preparation. We all learned arithmetic and how to read and write in school, but you'd be amazed at how many people get thrown by those 1040 forms. Bone up on the subject and early in the year announce that you're in the tax preparation business. Many giant firms began this way. They prove that there's no limit to how big *you* can grow. As the volume increases, merely add on assistants. True, it's seasonal—but it's also lucrative. One man I know works very hard for four months and then spends the other eight worrying about how to spend all that money.

4

How to Earn Big
Profits in Mail Order

Mail order has enabled more people to start on a shoestring and climb rapidly to wealth than practically any other field of endeavor. A home-based entrepreneur would be hard put to find a better means of earning large sums of money. The potential is staggering.

Take, for example, the experience a few years ago of a man who decided to try selling an automobile gadget and inserted a $225 ad in a national magazine. The ad pulled orders totalling nearly $5,000. He used the $5,000 to buy more ads in that and similar publications, and saw the first year's volume exceed $100,000.

But his story doesn't end there. With the experience and capital he had gained from selling that one item, he graduated into other specialty items. Today he runs one of the country's most prosperous catalog houses dealing in novelty merchandise. All with an out-of-pocket investment of $225!

WHY MAIL ORDER CAN BE YOUR
QUICKEST PATH TO WEALTH

When you do business by mail order you have a distinct advantage going for you—Uncle Sam. His Post Office Department serves as your store, your delivery boy, and your collection agent. He allows you to have a far wider horizon than, say, the corner grocer, who must add employees and cubic feet every time he wants to increase his volume.

Thanks to the post office, there are no boundaries to hold you back once you've established a winning product or service. Part of the receipts from your initial sales go into more advertising on a broader scale, and your profits can keep on multiplying indefinitely.

But how does someone just starting out know what type of products to choose—and where to advertise them? He makes his decisions following proven methods employed by virtually all successful mail order dealers. Adapting these methods to your own enterprise is the key to success, and that's what this chapter is all about.

HOW TO CHOOSE PROFITABLE PRODUCTS

You are soon to learn one of the key secrets of mail order success, one that is rarely found in the myriad of books, courses, and articles on mail order. It is a technique that has led many professionals to their most outstanding triumphs. And yet it is so simple, so basic, that most beginners ignore it. And that's their biggest mistake.

The secret is this:

The best way to select a profitable product is to choose one that is already being successfully sold by mail order.

So many people by-pass this important rule because they want to innovate. They want to be first on the market with something "hot." But they don't realize that few innovators are successful in mail order. For even if you were the first to introduce a product, and even if it were an outstanding seller, your exclusivity would be short-lived. Alert competitors would notice your success and move in.

Those alert competitors would be doing precisely what the rule tells them to do; they would be spotting your successful mail order item and taking steps to share in its success.

If, on the other hand, your "hot item" was a flop, your competitors would still be most grateful to you, because you would have borne all the expense of testing it on the market.

No, the mail order operator who is consistently successful lets others do the testing for him. He sells products that are well established.

Mail order is, by nature, an open book. You *know* what products and companies are successful because you see the ads repeated month after month, year after year. No one—not even the largest of firms— can afford to continue advertising something that is unprofitable to sell.

That's why a careful study of magazines—both current and back-copy—and a perusal of all the third-class mail you can get your hands on should be your very first move in preparing to go into mail order.

HOW TO ADVERTISE FOR TOP DOLLAR RESULTS

The shortcut for finding successful advertising media is the same as that for finding good products. You follow the leaders. You advertise in the media others are successfully using. If this type of advertising pays for them, the chances are excellent that it will pay for you. Never try to hide from the crowd and advertise in publications that have few mail order ads. There's a reason they have so few. These publications simply don't pull.

LEARN THE SECRET OF REPEAT SALES

Our discussion so far has been devoted to gaining customers. What do you do with them once the sale has been made—forget them? Never! Your biggest asset will be your customer list, and you will use it to make you rich!

It is far easier to sell to a customer who has purchased from you before than it is to sell to someone who has never heard of you. Tests have proven this time and again. The same sales piece, mailed to a "cold list" and to the house's own customer list, will pull five or even ten times as many orders from the house list.

In fact, many mail order houses willingly lose money on their first sale to a person just to get his name on their active list. Future sales to the same customer make up for the initial loss many times over.

So keep on going back to your customers with offers. Provided they were satisfied with their first purchase, your welcome will never be worn out.

Enough for the ground rules. Now for some specific routes that can lead you to your very own mail order pot o' gold.

Plan 1: SPECIALTY CATALOG

Some of mail order's leading success stories grew out of the specialty catalog business

In 1951, a man named Leonard Carlson launched a small mail order business on a shoestring. Its gross today is well up into the millions. You may have heard of this California firm. It's known as Sunset House.

A station agent at the express office in Redwood, Minnesota, saw an opportunity and latched onto it. A small package of watches arrived, addressed to a local jeweler. But the jeweler refused them. So, the station agent bought the watches and sold them to other agents along his line. Meeting with success, he bought more watches and sold them as well. Before long he quit his job and devoted full time to the mail order watch business. His name was Richard Sears. He later went into partnership with a man named Roebuck.

This is not to say that you will—or even wish to—become another Sunset House or Sears Roebuck. But certainly if two beginners could build the multi-million dollar enterprises just described, other beginners can earn steady and sizable incomes on a smaller scale.

FOLLOW THIS PROVEN METHOD

Basically, here's how you start and operate a successful specialty business:

1. Insert a display ad in a nationally-distributed publication known for its success in mail order sales.

2. As you ship each order to those who respond to the ad, include a catalog (which can be as small as a single page) advertising other products that might be of interest to the same person.

3. From time to time, as you prepare new catalogs, mail them to your customer list.

HOW TO SELECT YOUR PRODUCT LINE

The opening section of this chapter has given you the basic method for choosing the type of product to sell, and the closing section will provide some practical examples.

Other ideas, and specific product sources, can be found in the Journal of Commerce, published at 99 Wall Street in New York City. Various trade magazines will also be of great assistance. Go to a large public library and look up the "Business Publication Rates and

Data" edition of Standard Rate and Data Service. Here you'll find the names and addresses of various trade magazines in your field.

If you live in or near a big city, attend trade shows.

No matter where you live, you can do this: Look up all of the manufacturing plants within a radius of about 50 miles. Many of these firms will be happy to supply you with their products on order. And because you're local, you'll probably develop a much better business relationship than if you dealt with some industrial giant in a far-off metropolis.

HOW TO ADVERTISE

Send for the rate cards of each of the national magazines featuring ads for the type of product you wish to sell. In addition to providing advertising costs, these cards will give specific information on the preparation of ads. You'll note that most magazines are willing to set your ads into type for you so that you won't have to have mats or plates prepared.

Next, print up a catalog advertising your product line. It need not be a fancy one. To start, an 8½" × 11" sheet will do, as long as the items are attractively illustrated.

Then choose one item—the one you believe has the most sales appeal—and use it as your "lead." Advertise it in the magazines you have chosen.

As the orders come in, include your catalog with each shipment to a customer. Many customers will order additional items from the catalog, and noting the items that sell best will give you a good indication of what to include in future catalogs, and also what might make good "lead" items for future ads in the magazines.

You may even be surprised to learn that one of the catalog items is potentially a better seller than your original lead product. This is one of the fascinations of mail order. No one, not even the most experienced veteran, can always predict what will sell best.

WHAT ABOUT SYNDICATED CATALOGS?

If you've thumbed through any of the opportunity magazines, you've probably seen ads for syndicated catalogs. The firms publishing these are usually distributors who want you to sell their products for them. They provide you with the catalogs imprinted with your name. Some of these companies will even rent you mailing lists.

My advice is never to *base your business* on one of these catalogs. Think about it for a moment. With you and hundreds of other people mailing out the identical catalog to "cold" lists, how much chance do any of you have of succeeding?

But these catalogs can frequently be of value to you *after* you have built up your own list of satisfied customers—people who are willing and even anxious to purchase from you again. At this point, use of a syndicated catalog can provide an effective means of expanding your profit opportunities.

Plan 2: CLASSIFIED AD BUSINESS

There is no easier way to establish yourself in mail order than via classified ads. One little ad costing under $20 can reach millions of readers and result in sales in the hundreds of dollars.

Do some browsing at a newsstand and you'll find numerous national magazines with classified sections. You'll probably be surprised at the wide variety of products and services being sold.

A recent issue of Popular Science, for example, contains 82 different classifications, each with many different ads. It's obvious that hundreds of people are earning excellent incomes this way.

HOW THE SYSTEM WORKS

Very few products are sold directly from the ad. Its small size doesn't provide sufficient room for a convincing "pitch." What the classifieds do accomplish, and very successfully, is to whet the reader's appetite for more information.

And so, selling is a two-step process. The reader becomes interested in a product or service and sends away for literature on the subject. Then, hopefully, he responds by making a purchase.

This system provides the mail order dealer with a definite advantage. The literature he mails to inquirers is very similar to what other dealers send out to rented mailing lists, but in this case it is sent to people who have expressed a *definite interest* in the product or ser-

vice. They're known as "qualified prospects." They're much more apt
to buy than are people who have received unsolicited literature. A
rented mailing list does well if it results in sales to 2% of the recipients, while sales of 20% are not unusual when the same material is
sent to inquirers.

PREPARATION IS IMPORTANT

The first step in launching your own classified business is to study
the methods of those who are already established. Become an in-
quirer yourself, and write to all of the firms that offer free literature in
your chosen line. Before long you will have compiled an impressive
file of successful sales pieces.

Inspect this material very carefully. You'll find that in most cases it
consists of a one or two page letter accompanied by a single page
circular. The circular generally contains much the same information
as the letter, but it also includes illustrations or photographs to
increase the prospect's desire for what is being offered.

On the basis of the material you have received you can determine
whether you are equipped to prepare your own literature or whether
you should hire it done. A list of direct mail copy writers can be
found in the directory published in each issue of the trade magazine,
Reporter of Direct Mail Advertising. Subscription information is
available by writing to the magazine at 224 Seventh Street, Garden
City, N.Y. 11530.

HOW TO ADVERTISE

Once your literature has been prepared, you are ready to insert
your first classified ad. Most magazines carrying such advertising
publish information on rates, deadlines, and other requirements.
Magazines that don't publish such information will obligingly mail
you a rate card on request.

As for the writing of the ad itself, there's a basic rule. Due to the
fact that you pay on a "per word" basis, anything that can cut down
on the number of words without decreasing effectiveness is much to
be sought. Study some of the ads that run steadily and you'll see
economy at its best.

For example: "Send for a free brochure" can be cut from five to two words without losing any effectiveness. "Free brochure" says the same thing.

Start by inserting an ad in one magazine. Send out your sales literature to all who respond. Determine from the sales results what type of monthly profit you could expect if the ad were to run regularly. If the number of inquirers should be below the profit point, try revising the ad and inserting the new version in a future issue.

When you've hit upon the kind of ad that brings profitable response, begin using it in other magazines. You'll find that not all will pull equally well, but testing will lead you to a good number of magazines that do bring profitable results. Schedule a steady advertising program with each of these, and you can count on a consistent income month after month.

HOW WELL CAN YOU DO?

Let's take a hypothetical case that is typical of many classified business success stories. Suppose you are offering a tool kit that has a list price of $9.95. It costs you $5 to put it in the mail, and this includes wholesale price, postage, and packing, etc. You insert a $17.50 classified ad in a magazine, and you receive 116 inquiries. It then costs you 10¢ to mail literature to each of the inquirers. Fifteen per cent of those receiving the literature buy the tool kit. That amounts to 17 sales. Here's what your costs would be:

$17.50	classified ad
11.60	sales literature
85.00	merchandise
$114.10	total cost

Your receipts total $169.15 (17 × $9.95). Subtract the cost from this and you have a profit of $55.05. And that's from only one magazine. Eight ads per month on this basis can provide you with an average spare-time weekly income of $100.

Once your customer list reaches a suitable size, you can put together a small catalog of various other tools and increase your profits substantially.

Plan 3: BOOKS

Experts have long contended—and rightly so—that books comprise one of the best fields in which to operate a mail order business.

There are a number of reasons:

- Books are easy to handle and mail.

- Special postage rates give the book dealer a financial advantage.

- It's an excellent repeat-sale item; a customer who buys one book is very apt to purchase others on the same general subject.

- Thousands of titles are available, making the potential range virtually limitless.

This is not to say that *all* kinds of books are good mail order sellers. Few if any companies, except for the book clubs, have achieved success with fiction, for example.

And no matter what type of book you sell, you have to obtain it at a discount substantially larger than the 40% offered by most publishers. As a rule, that margin isn't large enough to provide for advertising, overhead, and profit.

The two primary elements of success, therefore, are: (1) choosing the right type of book, and (2) finding a low cost source. We'll deal with them in order.

WHAT BOOKS TO FEATURE

Non-fiction—especially instructional volumes or reference works—are excellent sellers through the mail. This would include anything that helps a person improve himself, advance in job or business, pursue a hobby, or obtain knowledge in a field in which he is interested.

The most important factor to consider in choosing your line of books is the "size of the audience." You must select a field in which a sufficiently large number of persons is interested. (Instructional tomes on how to repair carrousels would hardly be good candidates.)

It is also advisable to choose a field in which you have a personal interest and some knowledge. This will be valuable in making individual selections and in preparing your advertising.

Here's a rundown of many topics that are proven sellers:

Hobbies, arts and crafts, photography, cars, boats, airplanes, hunting, fishing, business opportunities, money-making ideas, cooking, outer space, psychology, self-help, religion, inspirational, sexology, science, home repairs, gardening, flowers, health, hypnotism, biography, nature, pets, sports, dieting, travel, high fidelity, occultism, astrology, art, private flying.

Once you decide on a field, *stick to it.* You can't sell hunting books to those who have bought flower books and expect to make a profit.

A LOW COST SUPPLY SOURCE

But where can you find books at a large enough discount to make them profitable sellers? The answer lies in what are known as "overstock" or "remaindered" books.

It is not rare for a publisher to print many more copies of a book than he manages to sell. As later releases come along, these books pile up in the warehouse. The publisher, more interested in moving his latest titles, stops promoting the earlier releases, and they continue taking up space. Before long, the publisher finds himself forced to dispose of them in order to make room.

He sells them in large lots to companies that specialize in remainders. These companies, in turn, wholesale them to book dealers. Many with an original price tag of $4.95, for example, are available for a dollar or less.

The dealers usually sell them to the public for $2 or $3. But *you* will be able to charge the full list price. Unlike the bookstores that purchase these volumes at random, you will feature one specific field of knowledge, and will be able to offer a variety of titles on that subject. To customers interested in the subject, this is a welcome convenience. They couldn't care less how you got your books, just as long as you have them.

Following is a list of some firms that sell overstock books to dealers. Write to each and request its latest wholesale catalog.

Book Sales Inc. 352 Park Ave. So., New York, N.Y. 10010	Wholesale Book Corp. 48-52 East 21st St., New York, N.Y. 10010
Overstock Book Co., Inc. 519 Acorn St., Deer Park, L.I., N.Y. 11729	World Wide Book Service 251 Third Ave., New York, N.Y. 10010

As each catalog arrives, check for the availability of titles in the field you've chosen. Bear in mind that not only do you need your "lead" book—but others for follow-up sales as well.

Let us suppose that your chosen field is travel and adventure. A recent catalog of a New York firm lists 32 books in that field—with $5.95 volumes available for 90¢, $1.95 books available for 30¢, etc. It's easy to see that you would not be at a loss for products to offer.

HOW TO BUILD A CUSTOMER BASE

An important decision is the selection of your initial book—the one with which you hope to attract customers. It should be of widespread appeal in the general field so that you will create a large customer base to which you can sell further volumes.

There are three ways to sell this initial book. One is by following the classified ad method outlined in the previous plan in this chapter. Another is direct mail, using the same type of literature that you send to persons who respond to your classified ads. Numerous mailing list brokers are listed in the directory published each month in the Reporter of Direct Mail Advertising. And the third method is the use of display ads in publications.

With each book you ship to a customer, you will include either a folio advertising another book in that field, or a small listing of *all* books you have available on the subject. These advertising pieces are called "stuffers" and they are an excellent, low cost means of obtaining added business.

Maintaining accurate records of all purchasers, you'll be able at regular intervals to send out material advertising the various additional titles you have to offer. This will be your prime source of profit.

How big can the profit be? It depends on the scale at which you choose to operate. Running a number of classified ads per month can generate enough business for monthly earnings of $300 or so; with the use of mailing lists to expand your growth you can draw ten times that amount.

Plan 4: DROP SHIPPING

Many people who would like to go into mail order hesitate to do so because they have visions of shelling out a large amount of money for stock and then having to find a place to store it until it's sold. They also fear that some of it *won't* be sold—and they'll be stuck with a thousand toothpaste tube-squeezers or some other such gadget.

Thanks to a system known as drop shipping, these worries need no longer be. It's possible never to touch, let alone store, one item that you're selling. And you don't pay for any merchandise until it has actually been ordered by a customer.

What is drop shipping? It's an arrangement you make with the manufacturer or distributor of a product to have it shipped directly to the customer from the factory or warehouse. As each order comes in, you prepare a shipping label and forward it, along with the wholesale cost of the product, to the drop shipper, and he handles the rest. Because he uses your label, it appears as though the shipment came from you.

Many of the largest mail order houses use this system for at least some of their products. It works well for them, and with proper planning it can work equally well for you.

THE KEY TO PRODUCT SELECTION

What types of products are drop shipped? Just about anything *can* be handled this way, but it's best to remember the basic mail order rule about featuring items that can be easily mailed, and at relatively low postage rates.

Novelty and gift items are probably your best bet. Many mail order dealers selling these products use drop shipping almost exclusively.

Product ideas and manufacturers' names and addresses can be obtained by following the trade journals, such as *Gift & Tableware Reporter, Gift & Art Buyer, Housewares Review,* and *Incentive.*

Attend trade shows, if possible. Follow up product ads you see in consumer magazines. If you see something in a store that you think might be a good mail order item, jot down the manufacturer's name and address. And don't overlook the firms in your own community. Sometimes all it takes is a telephone call to set up a mutually profitable arrangement.

HOW TO DEAL WITH THE MANUFACTURER

Unfortunately, not all firms will drop ship. Some are just not geared for it. But after locating a product you would like to handle, it's easy enough to determine this by corresponding with the manufacturer.

When making your inquiry, ask if the manufacturer can also supply you with promotional material. This can be in either of two forms:

1. *Circulars*. Many firms have printed circulars which can be used as part of your mailing piece. You pay a nominal amount to cover the cost of printing.
2. *Reproduction Proofs*. This is a sharp copy of a promotional sheet or circular which your printer can use in making an offset plate in preparing your own sales literature. Repro proofs allow you to adapt the material to your own needs.

A DISADVANTAGE OF DROP SHIPPING

Since the goods are sent out directly from the factory, you won't be able to include any stuffers or catalogs outlining the other items you have for sale. But it's not as big a problem as it appears. When you send your acknowledgment of the order to the customer, put the sales material in the same envelope. This way it still gets a free ride. (And it *is* imperative that you acknowledge each order as it's received. This is because of the delay involved in forwarding the order to the factory.)

HOW CATALOG FIRMS CAN BE HELPFUL

In Plan 1 of this chapter, I advised against basing a mail order business on the use of syndicated catalogs. All of these firms do function, however, on the drop ship system—and it's possible that you can work out an arrangement to offer some of their products in *your own* advertising.

For example, Terra Sancta Guild, 1019 Filbert, Philadelphia, Pa. 19107, offers—in addition to its 32-page catalog—what it calls "custom-made catalog sheets adapted for your market."

And, as explained in Plan 1, syndicated catalogs can be profitable after you have worked up your own customer list. Here are some other firms you might contact:

Benson-Maclean
Garden Catalog Service
Bridgeton, Ind.   47836

Brewster Service
627-629 Franklin St.,
Clearwater, Fla.   33517

Gift Guide
1137½ Crenshaw Blvd.,
Los Angeles, Cal.   90019

Giftime
919 Walnut,
Philadelphia, Pa.   19107

Graphic Publishers
1033 SW 53rd St.,
Oklahoma City, Okla.   73109

Sir Henry Morgan Ltd.
Castleton, Jamaica

Wilshire Mail Order Books
12015 Sherman Rd.,
N. Hollywood, Cal.   91605

Mail Order Methods
866 Flag Dr.,
Lafayette Hill, Pa.   19444

Value House
Direct Mail Div.,
663 Fifth Ave.,
New York, N.Y.   10022

55 MORE PRODUCTS AND SERVICES

Each of the following products and services is a top-selling mail order commodity. This list, although far from complete, will give you an indication of the broad range open to the person interested in entering this fascinating field.

The frequency with which these products and services are advertised proves that any one of them can provide an excellent basis for a highly profitable mail order enterprise.

Address labels
Advertising novelties
Amateur radio gear
Apparel

Army surplus
Art supplies
Auto supplies
Beauty supplies

Business calendars
Cameras
Camping supplies
Candy
Cigars
Clothing accessories
Coats of arms
Correspondence courses
Exercise equipment
Extension telephones
Fancy cheeses
Film developing
Fruitcakes
Gardening supplies
Gifts
Health foods
Health products
High fidelity equipment
Hobby items
Home decorative items
Investment advisory services
Jewelry
Kitchen utensils
Knickknacks

Ladies wigs
Luggage
Mailing list rental
Meat, frozen or smoked
Musical instruments
Newsletters
Office needs
Pet supplies
Phonograph records
Pipes
Religious items
Rubber stamps
Sewing accessories
Smoking accessories
Sports equipment
Stamps for collectors
Stationery
Stereo tapes
Tools
Toys & games
Unassembled furniture
Vitamins
Wrist watches

5

Producing Your Own
Top-Selling Items

A production center in your home? Why not? Thousands of people are drawing giant profits from what they manufacture, grow, raise, or otherwise produce in their homes.

There's no need for a lot of space. A table top or a corner of a room is often all that's required.

The field of opportunities is broad—from handcrafted items to living creatures. There's a huge market, thanks to the millions of people with a yen for that which is handmade or home grown.

ENJOY A PAYING PASTIME

"He has carried every point who has mingled profit with pleasure." The Roman poet, Horace, wrote that some 2,000 years ago. It is, of course, just as true today as it was then, with the proof provided by the many people who reap double benefits from their home production centers—the enjoyment of a hobby-type pursuit and the financial rewards of a thriving business. There's an added satisfaction, too, that comes from knowing that what you produce will be used and enjoyed by others.

Numerous businesses have been developed as extensions of what began as hobbies. The reverse is also true. It's not unusual to come across someone who launched an enterprise solely as a money-making venture only to find it so enjoyable that it developed into a hobby as well, albeit a very profitable one.

HOW TO CHOOSE A SUCCESSFUL PRODUCT

Reading this chapter will give you an excellent indication of the many types of products that can be created at home and successfully marketed. You'll learn what others have done and how they did it.

Perhaps, without realizing it, you already have a creative hobby that can be profitably merchandised. The following pages will give you a good idea of its profit potential, and how best to achieve that potential. Seeing how other people profited from their hobbies will help you capitalize on yours.

But having no such specialty at present is no drawback. There are six outstanding plans here that you can put into action just as they are or adapt to match your own abilities and circumstances. These are supplemented with a wealth of thought-provoking ideas that can lead to a lifetime of highly remunerative recreation.

FIVE EASY WAYS TO SELL YOUR OUTPUT

The ready market for home-created products is among the prime advantages of this type of business. There are five basic merchandising methods. Select one and you're on your way.

1. *Sell from Your Home*. Sometimes all it takes is a sign out in front. Take a drive in an area of private homes and you'll pass many with placards touting such specialties as maple syrup, rustic furniture, fishworms, evergreens, women's apparel, and garden produce—to name but a few. You may be surprised at the wide variety of products with which people are earning substantial spare-time cash.

2. *Consign to Stores*. Many retail establishments are eager to accept goods on a consignment basis. When the item is sold, the store deducts its commission, and you keep the rest.

3. *Mail Order*. Many a lucrative mail order business is based on products the dealer manufactures in his own home. In fact, a number of firms that are now in the big league got their start this way.

4. *Mail Order Wholesaling*. If you don't wish to handle the retail end yourself, perhaps your product can be sold to established mail order firms. These companies are constantly on the lookout for additional products to feature in their catalogs. You can rent a list of mail order houses from a broker, or you can compile your own list from the magazine ads featuring items similar to yours ·

5. *Classified Ads.* The "merchandise for sale" section in a local newspaper will often generate all the business you can handle. A brief description of your product should result in numerous phone calls from prospects anxious to go to your home and inspect what is being offered. Many of these people will become buyers and—if the product is a repeat-sale item—continual customers for years to come.

Plan 1: CUSTOM FRAMING

There's a man in a community outside Chicago who has an unusual display on his living room wall. It's a wooden frame that holds a ten-dollar bill behind a sheet of glass. If it were hanging in a store, barber shop, or barroom, the display might not seem so out of place, because it is common practice in such business establishments to frame the first piece of money received in income.

Actually, the man in Illinois is following this custom to the letter. His living room is where he transacts most of his business, and the ten-dollar bill is the first payment he received in an enterprise that has since earned him the equivalent of thousands more just like it.

But that's not all that makes it appropriate for Roy Farnsworth to hang a framed bill on his living room wall. The frame itself has a special significance. It is the item upon which his spare time enterprise is based. This businessman is a custom framer, and his field encompasses paintings, photographs, diplomas, mementos, and any number of other things his customers wish to display.

He entered the business several years ago without prior experience in or knowledge of the work. He received his "education" from literature available at a local art supply store, and his initial supplies were obtained there as well.

The degree of his success, and of others like him across the land, is a good indication of how profitable custom framing can be for people seeking part-time income at home.

BENEFIT FROM THE BOOM IN ART

Consider the market for a moment. There's a boom going on in original art, made possible by mass production methods that have put the price within everyone's reach. One supply firm, for example, employs five artists, each of whom colors up at least 15 pieces of canvas per day, accounting for a total company output of something like 18,000 paintings per year. They sell for about $25 each, and the quality is surprisingly good.

This art finds its way into homes, restaurants, hotels, offices, and apartment houses.

But the need for frames doesn't stop there. Photography enthusiasts seek suitable frames for their prize photos, doctors require enclosures for their medical degree certificates, hobbyists like to display their prime pieces; the list is virtually endless.

START WITH A MINIMUM OF EQUIPMENT

If you own a hammer, a saw, an electric drill, and a miter box, you're all set, thanks to the availability of pre-finished moldings. All you have to do is cut them to desired size, drill and brad their corners, and hand them over to a pleased customer who gives you an appreciative smile and up to $10. How much time has been involved? About a quarter of an hour.

Ready-made components will enable you to handle most of the work offered you. A retired man in Maryland clears about $50 per week this way, putting in just a few hours each day.

On the other hand, you can increase your versatility by adding on such luxury items as a tablesaw that will cut at angles for mitering particularly complex moldings, a portable saber saw for doing intricate work, and perhaps even a paint spray booth. But these pieces are not needed at the start and can be obtained from profits as your business grows.

A woman on the west coast began with pre-finished moldings and a small workbench in her basement. Her total investment for supplies and advertising was under $250. Gradually, as the need arose and the income made it possible, she added to her equipment and to her inventory. She now has quite an elaborate setup, and it has paid off. Her gross income amounts to $27,000 per year, and she reports that more than half is clear profit.

HOW TO OBTAIN CUSTOMERS

Your first step, of course, will be to order modest ads in the newspaper and in the Yellow Pages. You'll also want to have a small circular printed (it can be done for under $35) and distributed to such potential customers as art organizations, photo clubs, photographic equipment shops, and art supply stores.

Many custom framers have worked out arrangements with interior decorators. Those in your area will be glad to know of your service so that they can make use of it when carrying out their residential and commercial assignments.

ENJOY A BIG MARKUP

Your raw materials—molding, mat board, and mounting—will be a minor expense in comparison with what you'll receive for the finished work. Two or three dollars' worth puts together a $20 frame. The material for a simple project such as a diploma could cost as little as 50¢, and your charge would be as much as $5.

The profit need not be derived from frames alone. A logical way to expand is to sell paintings. Your home is a perfect gallery. Hang a few well-framed oils in strategic spots, and purchasers will be able to envision how they'd look in their own homes. You'll make sales that even the Main Street stores aren't able to achieve.

Plan 2: DOG BREEDING

"There's good money in mating dogs," says August Downing, and he should know. Last year his small business operation, conducted from a corner of his basement, pulled in more than $2,800. Thousands of others are enjoying comparable earnings, and the ones I've spoken with all have remarked about the amount of pleasure they derive along with their spare-time dollars.

Many of them, Gus included, got into the business quite by accident. Soon after Gus' wife returned home from the hospital following an operation, he decided that a puppy would be just the thing to cheer her up and keep her company during her convalescence.

After a poodle had been decided upon, he began shopping and found none available for under $100—and most for considerably more.

"This was a long way from the $25 I had expected to pay," Gus reports. "I quickly found that dog prices had jumped tremendously since I had been a kid. When I asked one breeder the reason for the high price in view of the relatively little cost to him, he explained that I was paying for a bloodline. This set me to thinking. If others could raise pups for profit, why couldn't I?"

And why not you, too? There's a big market not only for poodles, but for many other well-known breeds. German shepherds and Doberman pinschers, for example, are in great demand as guard dogs. A recent article in the *New York Times* noted that the demand for guard dogs is far outrunning the supply. Sales have jumped 50% to 100% in the last two years.

So, no matter which route you choose—pets or guard dogs—the market is there. Naturally, purchasers demand a pure strain, and the dogs must be bred for conformation and temperament, but meet these qualifications and you have a going business.

NO NEED FOR A PAIR

You can begin with just one dog—a female. Gus Downing started with the one he'd purchased for his wife. When the animal was about a year and a half old, he took her to a local kennel and for $125 employed the services of a stud dog. Some 60 days later a litter of four males and three females was born. Eight weeks after that, the males were sold for $150 each, and one of the females for $15.

Gus held on to two of the females for future breeding purposes. It cost under $300 per year to feed and care for each of the dogs. His only other expense was two or three hundred dollars for care of newborn pups, record-keeping, and advertising.

HOW TO BEGIN

Step number one in launching a dog-breeding enterprise is to give yourself some education on the subject. Just about everything you'll need to know is contained in the official publication of the American Kennel Club, *The Complete Dog Book*. It's available at most book stores. In it, you'll find information helping you to choose the best breed for you, and valuable advice on care, training, breeding, and whelping.

When the time for stud arrives, you can obtain advice from the breeder who sold you your dog or from your veterinarian. You can also get some excellent leads by attending local dog shows and learning firsthand what lines are producing the best new stock.

Owners of stud dogs are interested in producing offspring that will bring credit to them as well as to you, and this is where you'll find that your own dog's pedigree will be helpful. If there are champions in the immediate background, all to the good. And it would be commercially to your advantage to arrange stud with a male that has achieved his own championship. You'll get better prices for your pups when you can say the sire was a champ.

Standards of the American Kennel Club are accepted universally in the United States. Your mating dogs will, of course, be registered with the AKC, and as soon as whelping occurs, your litter should be, too. Papers for registering a litter can be obtained by writing the AKC at 51 Madison Avenue, New York, New York 10010. As each pup is sold, it should be individually registered with the AKC.

HOW TO BRANCH OUT

You'll soon find it is possible to make money from any of several sidelines related to the selling of puppies. One is the sale of supplies such as leashes, collars, brushes, dog beds, name tags, etc. Another is maintaining facilities to board the dogs you've sold when the new owners go on vacation.

As you become more familiar with the canine world, such services as grooming and training may also be developed as profitable sidelines.

These activities can eventually lead to a full-fledged kennel operation, if this is to your liking. Or your efforts can be held to a minimum spare-time pocket-money enterprise. It all depends on your goals and the space and time you have available.

Plan 3: ACCESSORIES AND KNICKKNACKS

Can you still base a business on handmade articles and hope to compete with what comes off production lines?

Certainly!

Because most of what is in the marketplace today *is* mass-produced, the items that reflect true individual craftsmanship attract larger throngs of buyers than ever before.

Starting with just a few raw materials, you can help serve this market and at the same time develop a lifelong source of extra income.

And there's no reason to be held back by the belief that you have no particular skills that would fit such an enterprise. You do have the ability, latent though it may be, and all you need do is discover and develop it.

Mrs. Pearl Daniels of Grafton, Massachusetts, discovered hers quite by accident. It began one Christmas season when the Daniels family was in such poor financial shape that she had no money with which to buy presents for the children of her friends. Calling on the ingenuity that such straits frequently create, Mrs. Daniels reached into her ragbag and began making dolls with flesh-tinted material stuffed with cotton. They were an immediate hit with the young recipients and their mothers. They clamored for more, and were willing to pay for them.

Here was an opportunity, and Mrs. Daniels grabbed it. If the dolls were popular in Grafton, why not elsewhere? Advertisements in regional publications proved she was right. The doll business came to be the chief financial support of her family, and succeeding Christmases were far more bountiful.

Millard Neal of Biddeford, Maine, had no intention of going into business when he made his first decorative neckerchief slide for use on a Boy Scout uniform. Mr. Neal had been active in Scout work, and turning out slides for some of his Scouts seemed at first to be merely an enjoyable hobby.

Some hobby! The slides caught on so rapidly that he began to set a price for them and then had to employ helpers to turn them out. Before long, production reached 150,000 units per year.

There are thousands of items to choose from in launching your own accessory and knickknack business, and if you pay heed to the guidelines that follow there's every reason to expect outstanding financial rewards.

HOW TO CHOOSE YOUR PRODUCT

It has been demonstrated time and again that there are four categories of handmade articles that top the list of best-sellers. Choose one (or even a combination) and you'll have a head start in meeting your profit goal.

Native Materials. The use of materials native to your area will give your product the advantage of being sought after by tourists as mementos of their visit, and by others as something that typifies that particular region.

Maine, for example, is noted for its large wooded areas and its seacoast, and both played a big role in supplying Dick and Ruth Jackman of Fayette with their raw materials. Their first items were earrings fashioned from acorns. Next came other types of accessory items, made with pine cones and various seeds. The business expanded from jewelry to household items, including lamps formed from driftwood, with orders arriving from all corners of the land.

Unusual Materials. Frequently, the introduction of an uncommon element into what would otherwise be a common product can spell outstanding success.

Who, for instance, would think of granite as the "gem" on such items as cufflinks and tie clasps? Dr. DeForest Jarvis of Barre, Vermont, did, and the finished product soon became popular with tourists stopping at gift shops located throughout the Green Mountain State. Dr. Jarvis (who, incidentally, wrote the best-selling book, *Folk Medicine*) sliced the granite into small, thin pieces and placed it atop silver mountings. Its unusual popularity was caused by its unusual nature.

Unusual Design. This can spell the difference between the mediocre and the exceptional in terms of both product and profit. Take such an ordinary thing as a book end, give it an unusual design, and your prospects have been greatly enhanced.

Or take hooked rugs. Unusual designs have become the specialty of those made by Miss Martha Batchelder at Hampton Falls, New Hampshire, for people who like to adorn their homes with such original creations. Many women have made hooked rugs, but few have strayed from the more orthodox patterns. Miss Batchelder did, and profited handsomely because of it.

Useful Purpose. Make your product utilitarian—perhaps even more so than what is currently on the market—and you have a solid base for a profitable enterprise.

Mrs. Elsie Farrell of Randolph, Massachusetts, found a good

market when she began making potholders that had an extra capacity
to hold out the heat—something that had been troubling housewives
for centuries. The heat-resistant nature of her product is caused by
the fact that each potholder has six layers of flannel. Mrs. Farrell
found an important need and filled it.

HOW TO CHARGE

When setting the price for what you produce, don't neglect to take
your time into account. If an item takes an hour to produce, you've
got to figure a good one hour's wage for yourself *in addition to* a
reasonable profit margin and your out-of-pocket expenses.

If it's a relatively small-ticket item, your production methods have
to be quick and efficient. Mr. and Mrs. Bill Shevis of Belmont,
Maine, succeeded in doing this in their business featuring colorfully
designed handkerchiefs. The design is transferred by the silk screen
method, and this has allowed the Shevises to turn out these fine items
in rapid enough order to be well paid for their time.

Naturally, some handmade items take quite a while to produce.
The skill or artistry involved makes them *worth* it, and their prices
should be set accordingly. In Stone County, Arkansas, a resident who
is adept at wood carving runs a roadside shop at which his output is
offered for sale. He uses walnut, sassafras, cherry, hackberry, and
other native woods to carve many varieties of animals and birds.
Customers are attracted to his shop from miles around, and they
willingly pay for the time and ability that have gone into his work.

HOW TO DETERMINE YOUR SALES METHOD

This is best explained by giving two examples.

Mrs. Cora Jo Fabiyan has proven that if you have a popular
product, people will flock to your home, no matter the location. This
resident of Hampton Beach, New Hampshire, makes doll clothing.
Her home is located at the end of a dead-end road in a remote area,
but people come from far and wide to see and buy her handiwork.

Bill Jennings of Chicago weaves thin pieces of wood into tiny
baskets that serve as pencil and letter holders. Realizing that people
rarely go out shopping for an item such as this—but will often buy it

on impulse—he's arranged to have a number of Illinois stores handle it on consignment. The plan has worked out well, with the stores easily disposing of all that Mr. Jennings can produce.

If, as is the case with Mrs. Fabiyan, your product is unique and much in demand, you can draw customers to *you*. On the other hand, if items of a similar nature are commonly available, follow Bill Jennings' lead and go to the customers.

Plan 4: DRAPERIES

A skill that many women have and others can develop is the making of custom draperies. With a modest investment, this skill can be the source of excellent income. By no means are men excluded, because some of the most successful drapery services are owned and operated by members of the stronger sex.

No big outlay for a stock in materials is required. The fabric is purchased from the wholesaler as each job is received, or else it is provided by the customer. On the average, you can expect that your profit will be 40% of your gross receipts.

HOW TO BEGIN

Naturally, your first step will be to review your skill. If you've had experience in making drapes and feel confident that you can handle most of the jobs offered you, you're all set.

If you've had little or no experience, you'll either have to receive training or arrange for the services of someone who *is* skilled.

Your best bet would be to learn the field yourself. One of the easiest ways is probably to take a home study course such as the one offered by the Custom Drapery Institute, Box 555, Orange, Cal. 92669. Write to them for a free booklet outlining their instructional program.

Lacking the necessary skills, it's possible to go into partnership with someone else who is equipped to handle the job. You, then, would take care of the administrative and sales details, splitting the profits with your partner.

As for the equipment, a good sewing machine is, of course, necessary, along with the other appurtenances of the trade such as scissors, tape measures, etc. You'll also need a car so that you can go to your customers' homes or places of business to take measurements and complete the installation.

HOW TO OBTAIN CUSTOMERS

Most of your work will be done in homes and apartments, but offices, restaurants, and other commercial locations will also be good sources of business and should not be overlooked.

Your prime means of reaching the people who own or occupy these places will be advertisements in the classified section of the newspaper and in the Yellow Pages.

Real estate agents can also be helpful. With the promise of a small commission, you can have them provide you with leads when homes or apartments change hands. You might consider sending a circular to professional people, explaining how you can help make their offices more attractive.

It shouldn't be long before you'll be getting added business by word of mouth—with satisfied customers informing their friends of your service.

FINANCIAL ARRANGEMENTS

The fee for a good proportion of your jobs will run into several hundreds of dollars. The easier you make it for your customers to pay this, the more business you'll get. You can make an arrangement with one of the nationally-known bank-sponsored charge card systems. Your customers would then be able to use the charge card to delay or extend payments if they choose. You, of course, would get the money promptly from the card company. The cost to you would be the fee that the banks deduct. It's usually about 5%, and worth it in terms of the increased business the arrangement generates.

HOW TO EXPAND

Your work need not be limited to draperies. Custom slipcovers provide a natural means of increasing your volume. And this could eventually lead to a full line of interior decorating services.

As the amount of work grows, you can hire employees to do much or all of the work—with you devoting your time to conferring with customers and developing more business.

This is the kind of enterprise in which, working alone on a part-time basis, you should be able to earn up to $75 per week. It goes without saying that your earnings can jump to a much higher figure when and if you decide to go full time and/or hire one or more staff members.

Plan 5: TROPICAL FISH

The fact that there are thousands upon thousands of tropical fish enthusiasts who are in it for enjoyment alone proves that this is a profit plan that can be a lot of fun to carry out. The combination of fun and money is hard to beat.

As a breeder of tropical fish, your market will be the many others who pursue it merely as a hobby. You sell to them in either of two ways: directly, with the customers coming to your home to pick out what they want, or indirectly, through fish and pet stores in your area. Upon occasion, you'll even be able to sell some specimens to whole-sale houses that seek to add to their breeding stock.

LEARN THE RUDIMENTS

Unfortunately, a neophyte can't go out, buy some tanks, begin breeding fish, and hope to set up a profitable undertaking. It takes preparation in the form of educating yourself to the peculiarities of fish breeding and maintenance. But you can get that knowledge at your public library or a book store. Herbert R. Axelrod's *Tropical Fish as a Hobby* (McGraw-Hill) is your best bet. In it you'll find more information than you need on bringing fish into this world and keeping them here. Also recommended is *Breeding Tropical Fish* by the same author.

SPACE IS NOT A MAJOR REQUIREMENT

A corner of one room is all you need at first, provided the room is heated. Many breeders place their tanks on racks, one above the other, thereby minimizing the floor space. You'll need three types of tank—one for breeding stock, another for use in spawning, and the third to hold the stock that is to be sold.

Each tank will also need aeration and filter pumps, heating elements, gravel, and probably some plants. You can set up five tanks for about $200 as a starter and purchase more as the business develops.

Most experts agree that it is best to begin with just one species of fish, specializing in that until your knowledge and experience warrant some diversification. Because of their relative hardiness and well known reproductive abilities, guppies would be a good type to begin with. Later you can move on to the more rare, and consequently more profitable, varieties.

The wholesale price you'll collect will range from a nickel for guppies to a couple of dollars for their more rare cousins.

SELLING YOUR STOCK

While selling to individuals from your home can provide some spare-time cash, you'll find the big money is in selling in quantity to stores. Check the Yellow Pages for all pet shops in your area and visit, call, or write each of them, outlining what you have to offer. Discuss each store owner's needs with him, for this will help you determine what species to add to your stock in the future.

HOW ONE COUPLE DID IT

Mr. and Mrs. Harold Muller began by selling tropical fish at retail from their home. Since they live in an area in which there are not many pet shops, they reasoned that selling at retail would provide them with the best profit opportunities. They were right; their business grew to the point where they decided to open a fish and pet shop of their own in a local shopping center. It prospered, and after a few years they sold it at a handsome profit.

Their initial investment was $275. After that, every cent they used for expansion came from income. In addition to earning good profits each year they were in business, they walked away from their store, after having sold it, with a check well into the five figures.

Plan 6: WOOD PRODUCTS

If you've got a small woodworking shop or room for one, along with a few relatively inexpensive power tools, there's good money to be made in turning out products made of wood.

The secret for the one-man enterprise is to concentrate on *one* product and then develop some assembly-line techniques that will allow you to produce it in sufficient volume to draw a good profit. This by no means negates earlier statements in this chapter that the advantage of home-produced items is their superiority over those that are mass-produced. What you produce will be the result of individual craftsmanship *combined with* some of the techniques of high volume output.

An example: Fred Krueger specializes in making small magazine racks for the home. There are three slanted and tiered shelves on each side. Eight pieces of wood go into making the rack—the six shelves, and the two sides that support them. But there are only two *different* parts; the shelves are all alike and the two sides match each other. So, once a week, Fred spends several hours cutting out those two basic parts for his magazine rack—providing himself with enough material to handle all of the production of the following five days.

Because he makes only one product, and because he's adopted mass production methods, Fred can turn out enough in his spare time to earn, on the average, $65 per week. The items are sold by mail order and through local curio shops and even a few furniture stores.

HOW MUCH INVESTMENT IS REQUIRED?

This, of course, depends on the nature of your product. Your biggest outlay will be for a power saw, power drill, and the required hand tools. A few hundred dollars should do it. Naturally, the simpler your product, the less cash investment you need to make for equipment.

Wood and finishing materials will not be a major factor in setting up your shop, because you'll purchase "as you go"—replenishing your supplies as your existing stock is sold.

A BIG MARKET FOR PERSONALIZED ITEMS

There's a one-man shop in Pennsylvania from which the proprietor derives an excellent income by making rustic lawn signs. You've seen them and perhaps even have one on your own lawn—they consist merely of a small board with ragged edges on which reflective lettering has been tacked. These are stuck into the ground by means of a strip of iron to which they are attached.

The cost-to-produce (including wood, metal, and the purchase of the letters) is about three dollars, and the signs sell for twice that and up, depending on size.

Initial business was obtained by placing samples in hardware stores. Customers left deposits and picked up the finished material about a week later. More recently, arrangements have been made with several mail order houses to include the item in their catalogs. As the orders are received, the mail order firms deduct their commissions and forward the balance to the shop. When each sign is completed, it's mailed directly to the customer.

HOW TO CHOOSE A PRODUCT

The decision on what *you* will make depends on several things. If you have little woodworking experience, very small space for a shop, and don't wish to invest much for tools, lean toward a simple item—such as lawn signs, bird houses, trays, etc.

With more space, additional equipment, and ample experience you can go for the more elaborate items that boast higher price tags. These would include cabinets, record racks, chests, even hi-fi enclosures.

USE CARE IN SETTING THE PRICE

At first, you'll have to be a time and efficiency expert if you want to establish a price that will amply repay you for your costs and labor. The best way you can do this is to produce a small quantity of your product, working by the clock. Then sit down with pencil and paper, figure out your total time per item, and add the cost of materials, electricity, etc.

Next, add about 10% for other overhead expenses (to cover such matters as your time spent on administrative details), and finally, include a profit margin. Your labor, which was figured in earlier, is not part of the profit. The purpose of going into any business is to make a profit in addition to wages. If all you want to do is get paid for your time, you might as well hire on with someone else and let them take the business risk.

HOW TO EXPAND

If your product is a good one, you'll be able to sell all you produce through local stores, mail order ads, or through mail order companies. Any expansion will probably have to involve the hiring of helpers. This would allow you to explore *related* items, eventually working up a line of similar wood products.

This way, and by means of developing a mail order or wholesale catalog, there is virtually no limit to how big your business can grow.

16 OTHER PRODUCTS YOU CAN CREATE AND SELL

Garden Produce. Housewives can buy all of the vegetables and fruits they need at the corner supermarket, but rarely do they get the quality you can provide with your home-grown produce. You can get a whole summer's worth of income by featuring products that are in season at different times. Sales are easy; a table and a cardboard sign at roadside are all you'll need.

Worms. Fish bait can provide good spare-time cash. A good book on the subject from the library will give the information you need to start. In addition, there are firms that provide initial stock and instructions. Check the national classifieds.

Floral Arrangements. You don't have to own a florist shop to enter this business. You can specialize on weddings or social gatherings and charge competitive prices because of your lower overhead. Your "raw materials"—the flowers—can be purchased from wholesale firms.

Custom-Made Clothing. Making clothes to order is the basis of many one-man (or, usually, one-woman) enterprises. Dress designing is particularly remunerative. There are home study courses on this if you feel you need more training or experience. Or sign up for an adult education course in your local school system.

Parts for Manufacturers. Most factories are merely assembly plants; the parts are brought in. It's estimated that there are several hundred persons in the United States who draw substantial incomes by fabricating small components for major manufacturers. It's a specialized field, but by studying the trade journals and their want ads you could very well hit on a long-time source of spare or even full-time income.

Lamps from Unusual Items. Is there anything they *don't* make lamps out of these days? You can either initiate your own products from whatever your ingenuity comes up with, or you can launch a lamp-making *service,* with materials supplied by customers. Many people collect driftwood, buy old jugs, etc., for the eventual purpose of electrifying the stuff, but never get around to it. An ad in the paper should have many of them taking advantage of your service.

Lawn Decorations. From carved birds and small woodland animals to religious objects—there's good income to be earned from forming and selling lawn items. Sales are accomplished either through a shop in your home or by consigning to stores.

Rustic Furniture. Outdoor rustic furniture and such indoor items as coffee tables built from large hardwood slabs and chairs with cowhide or reed seats find a ready market in many areas. Since much rustic furniture is made from round stock of small size, material can be obtained from sawmill discards, woodland thinnings, or improvement cuttings.

Parakeets. The demand for good parakeets never seems to let up. With a breeding operation in your home, you can provide the quality that is missing in most birds coming from bulk hatcheries. Accordingly, many pet shops will be happy to purchase from you.

Magazine Art. Ever notice the excellent color plates in magazines and think what a shame it is that they're thrown out when the next month's issue comes along? Well, *don't* throw them out. You can make good money by pasting them to adequate pieces of wood and coating with a clear acrylic varnish. You can collect $2.50 for the smaller ones, more as the size increases.

Fireplace Wood. If you've got some woodland—or can arrange to make use of a neighbor's property—good cash is available by cutting up seasoned hardwood to fireplace size and delivering it to homes. A farmer in eastern Virginia gets $30 per face cord, and most of the wood comes from cull trees removed to improve the timber. Some entrepreneurs bundle or box fuelwood for sale at grocery stores, filling stations, and other retail businesses.

Flavor Woods. A business related to the above is the type that provides so-called "flavor" woods and chips for barbecue purposes. Among the most popular species used for this purpose are hickory, maple, cherry, apple, and oak.

Nursery Trees. A relatively small area of clear land is all you need, along with some seedlings purchased from a mail order nursery. Let them grow until they reach a foot or two in height, then advertise them on a "dig your own" basis. By setting out new trees each year, you'll have a year-in, year-out income with surprisingly little work.

Printing. A hand-operated printing press can be purchased for under $100, and with it you can turn out business cards, tickets, stationery, and other items that are always needed by individuals, clubs, and business organizations. By specializing in one or two items, no large array of type will be needed, frequent form changes won't be required, and you can work up a fine source of profit.

Metal Working. All kinds of useful and attractive things can be produced by the person who is handy with metal tools. Using such materials as copper, brass, or pewter, you can make letter openers, book ends, picture frames, trays, bowls, or mugs. Sell them from your home or place them in gift shops—you'll be well paid for your effort.

Pottery. Gift shops are also on the lookout for attractive pottery pieces. Working with clay and a kiln takes some practice, but this type of learning is fun and the end result can be profitable indeed.

Launching a Lucrative Repair Service

The key to a surprisingly high income is yours if you like to work with your hands and find that you've got a flair for fixing things. Although being an expert in a specific field certainly helps, it's far from essential. Picking up the necessary skills is easier than you might think.

CASH IN ON THE AFFLUENT SOCIETY'S FASTEST GROWING NEED

We live in a possession-mad world. People have more conveniences, appliances, and gadgets than ever before. And as you've learned from personal experience, anything with moving parts is subject to breakdowns. Few people have the skill, tools, or patience to repair these items when they do break down, preferring to send them out to a specialist.

Never was the need for such specialists as great as it is now—thanks to the affluence that allows the average family to acquire more and more possessions.

Thumb through your classified telephone directory and you'll see the wide variety of repair specialties that are the basis for business enterprises, many of them operated from home. Practically all of these—and some not listed—provide an opportunity for you.

YOU CAN BE A SPECIALIST STARTING FROM SCRATCH

Provided you are adept at fixing things *in a general way,* you can learn the particular skills required for the repair specialty you choose. Sometimes all it takes is a little practice, using an old or discarded item to work with. Other times you may need the assistance of an instructional book to guide you over the unfamiliar spots.

And in cases where really specialized knowledge is required, you have at your call a wide variety of home study and adult education courses. Any mechanics magazine contains scores of ads for home study schools. A telephone call to your local school system or the nearest college will reveal the availability of classroom training in your chosen field.

DOUBLE-BARRELED PROFITS
FROM PARTS AND SERVICE

Your repair enterprise will provide you with a profit advantage that not many other types of business offer. In addition to the excellent hourly income you'll derive from the work you do, you'll receive top profits from the *replacement parts* used in carrying out that work.

Your profit margin on these replacement parts will be at least 40%, and in many cases more. A part for which you pay $4.20, for example, brings you at least $7.00. Thus, a typical repair job that takes less than an hour to complete might carry a total charge of $15. This includes $8 for your labor, $4.20 as your cost for the part, and $2.80 as your profit for the part. This means you've earned $10.80 for the job. That's hard to beat for an hour's work.

Now let's examine some of the high-paying repair specialties that can be successfully conducted from your home.

Plan 1: APPLIANCE REPAIRING

If you've ever had a household appliance break down and have tried to get a technician to repair it promptly, you know the problem that exists. With the large number of appliances in use today, repairmen have much more than they can handle.

This may be bad for the consumer, but it's mighty good news for you, because here is a field with a built-in need. There's probably not a medium-sized community in the United States that couldn't use another appliance repair service.

LEARN FROM THE MANUFACTURERS

How do you get started? If you've had some experience fixing appliances for yourself or friends, probably all you need do is some boning up. Most manufacturing companies put out a manual listing all of the products made by them each year. These manuals include parts lists and instructions for repair and overhaul. They'll provide the familiarization you need as you get started, and they'll be useful guides when jobs start coming your way.

You'll probably find that dealing with the nearest wholesale parts distributing firm is much more convenient than purchasing parts from the individual manufacturing firms. You'll want to become familiar with the service the distributor offers—such as the time it takes to get needed parts into your hands and how shipment is accomplished.

If you feel you need additional training in appliance repair, there are a number of home study schools. Here are three from which you can obtain descriptive catalogs:

> National Radio Institute
> Appliance Division
> 3939 Wisconsin Ave.,
> Washington, D.C.   20016

> National Schools
> 4000 South Figueroa St.,
> Los Angeles, Cal.   90037

> International Correspondence Schools
> Scranton, Pa.   18515

When you write to these schools, be sure to specify that you are interested in appliance repair, as a number of other courses are taught by each institution.

HOW TO SET PRICES

Since practically every job you handle will be different, the only basis on which you can establish your charge is time-plus-parts. Set an hourly wage for yourself—a figure that is divisible by four so that you can break each job down to the nearest quarter hour. If, for example, your wage is $8 per hour and a job takes an hour and a quarter to complete, the labor charge would be $10.

If you do work "on location," i.e., at the customer's home or office, the labor charge would be portal to portal—the clock starts when you leave home and doesn't stop until you return. Some servicemen boost their hourly rate slightly to cover the cost of transportation.

If you make a lot of house calls you can establish a fee that covers the call and up to about one-half hour at the location.

GIVE A GUARANTEE

You must stand behind your work. If it proves defective within a specified period, you agree to correct it free of charge. The guarantee period is usually anywhere from 30 to 90 days. Be sure to mention the guarantee in your advertising, and to write it out on the receipts you give your customers. It's a powerful business-creator.

Speaking of creating business, you'll probably be surprised at how easy it really is. Word of mouth with your neighbors, co-workers, and friends will provide a good start, along with a classified in the paper and an insertion in the Yellow Pages. Once the word gets around that there's a good serviceman who actually *welcomes* additional work, your income-producing hours will be full.

EXPAND FOR GREATER PROFITS

As you progress, various methods of expansion will become obvious to you. One is to move the business out of your home and into a store in a downtown area or shopping center. If your wife has her days free, she might serve behind the counter while you hold down your regular job; you'd do the repair work at night. Later, a clerk could be hired, preferably one who is mechanically inclined, or you might find it more feasible to take on the operation full-time yourself.

Other services can be provided in the store. Successful sidelines include key-making, sales of parts and kits for do-it-yourselfers, garden tools, etc.

Whether you continue to operate from home or move to a store, there are some "percentage" activities from which you may be able to profit. Even if you have no knowledge of electronics, you'll be able to take radio and phono repair jobs because almost any local radio-TV service will be glad to handle your work on a commission basis. You get to keep 10 or even 20 per cent of the charge. Other specialized fields in which you can farm out work include electric motor repair, large appliance jobs, and lawnmower overhaul service.

Plan 2: FURNITURE REFINISHING

Whether it's early American or modern Grand Rapids, quite a lot of furniture sooner or later reaches the point where it needs to be refinished and/or reupholstered. Providing this service can be a highly satisfying type of work, and well paying, too.

Gerald Osborn is an Illinois resident who is typical of the many people who conduct highly successful furniture renewal enterprises at home. What's his secret of success? Why do people go to him rather than a big shop?

"I think it's mostly psychological," he explains. "Naturally, I do good work and I do it at reasonable prices. But so do many of the shops. It seems that people like doing business with an individual, one who works at home and takes pride in giving careful attention to what he does. They think they're dealing with an old-time craftsman, I suppose."

He does a small amount of advertising, but finds that most of his new business comes from referrals from satisfied customers.

NO SPECIAL TRAINING REQUIRED

Do there continue to be opportunities for others wishing to start out in the field?

"Definitely," is his reply. "And you need not be a genius at wood-working, either. A few simple tools, some practice, and a little patience—that's all it takes. If people only knew how simple the basic procedure is, they'd be redoing their own furniture. But they don't, and that's why just about anyone who sets himself up as a professional can make a go of it . . . provided he gives quality at fair prices."

Mr. Osborn learned of its profit potential quite by accident. The factory where he worked was hit by a strike and he found himself with an abundance of time and a lack of money. With thousands of others in the same predicament, there were no temporary jobs available. Rather than twiddle his thumbs until the strike ended, Osborn decided to make use of some old hand tools he had in the basement and refurbish the ancient bedroom set that he and his wife had purchased from a second hand store when they were married.

It was strongly built, he reasoned, and would be entirely serviceable for a number of years to come if only its appearance didn't reveal its age. It was chipped and scratched, and its design was outmoded.

The night table was the smallest piece in the set, so he began with that, with the plan of working up to the larger pieces as he gained experience. Mr. Osborn chiseled off the scroll decorations, removed the knob on the drawer, applied some varnish remover, and used sandpaper to get down to the basic wood.

Then, following the instructions that came with refinishing material he had obtained at the hardware store, he proceeded to give the table its new coating. Later, when it was dry, a brass knob was attached as a replacement for the one that had been removed, and, behold, Osborn had "created" a night table that had the appearance of being fresh out of the store.

His wife was so pleased that she urged him to move ahead rapidly to the remaining pieces in the set—the bureau, a dresser, and the bed.

When the job was done, the Osborns had a "new" bedroom set for the cost of a small quantity of stain and some brass fittings, plus a few hours of effort.

A BUSINESS IS BORN

It wasn't long before a neighbor persuaded Osborn to do a kitchen set. Keeping the price low because he considered himself an amateur, he gained confidence as the job progressed.

Doing the work for the neighbor caused other people to badger him to do similar jobs for them.

"I realized that I really didn't know that much about it, but since it had been fun and profitable, I picked up some books on the subject at the library. I particularly wanted to know about reupholstery, since this is what many people seemed interested in."

At about that time the strike at his factory ended, and he went back to work. But he spent many of his free hours learning all he could about his new spare-time trade, and he invested about $100 in tools to augment what he already had.

He found that as his knowledge increased, so did the speed of his work. And he was able to predict approximately how long any given job would take. This allowed him to offer price-quotes as he began to take on an increasing number of outside jobs.

A HUSBAND AND WIFE TEAM

Mrs. Osborn became just as enthused in the budding enterprise as her husband, and took on the job of making slipcovers and draperies. She also helped with the reupholstering.

Before long, profits from the sideline enterprise were averaging more than $50 per week. It became obvious that if Osborn were to devote full time to the project, he could earn double what he was drawing from the factory. And this would mean less total hours worked (no burning the midnight oil), no problems with strikes or layoffs, and no worry about getting to or from work on bad weather days.

Ex-factory worker Gerald Osborn is now a very active full-time furniture-renewer.

There are still jobs that he does not feel he can handle adequately, and this work is passed on to a woodworking shop in his neighborhood. He receives a commission for this.

He has expanded the scope of his enterprise somewhat by buying certain types of furniture to be refinished and resold. He specializes in Victorian sofas and chairs. Several hours of work can make a piece he bought for $25 sell for $75 or more.

HOW YOU CAN MAKE MONEY IN FURNITURE RENEWAL

If Gerald Osborn's experience sounds as if this is a field that would interest you, your first move will be to develop your proficiency. If you want to speed up the process, register for an adult ed course in a nearby school system.

You may, however, prefer to take the route Osborn followed and train yourself. With perhaps the aid of a book or two, practice on several pieces of old furniture rescued from the attic or purchased in a junk shop. As with Osborn, you'll probably be surprised at how simple the refinishing procedure really is.

You may want to include reupholstering as one of your services, and for this it would probably be advisable to take one of the several home study courses advertised regularly in the mechanics magazines.

In all likelihood, once the word gets out that you are in the furniture renewal business your friends and their friends will give you all the jobs you can handle. This is how Osborn got started. You can, of course, spur things on with a newspaper ad or two and a listing in the classified directory.

Plan 3: HI-FI DOCTOR

There are two basic requirements for this one. You've got to be a high fidelity/stereo enthusiast, and you have to have a knowledge of electronics. If you pass muster (and it's safe to say that hundreds of thousands of people do) you can profitably become a "doctor of high fidelity."

A doctor without degree, to be sure; but a doctor whose practice can be more interesting than a surgeon's, less demanding than a specialist's, and perhaps more profitable on an hour-by-hour basis than a general practitioner's. How many medical men average $45 per house call?

WHY HI-FI OWNERS NEED YOU

The tremendous popularity high fidelity has achieved is the reason behind the success of a growing number of enterprises based on servicing hi-fi and stereo equipment. Most radio and TV repair shops are unqualified and ill-equipped for this type of service, and owners of high fidelity and stereo equipment must look to specialists to keep it in shape.

Because most home music systems are comprised of separate

components rather than single integrated units, it is usually inconvenient for the owner to haul the entire system into a shop for repair. Thus, high fidelity repair specialists do a good deal of their work in the homes of their customers.

MEET THE HI-FI DOCTOR

A successful operator of just such an enterprise is William Bohn of New York City, who, aptly enough, gained a reputation throughout that metropolis as "The Hi-Fi Doctor." He answers house calls from people with stuttering stereos, temperamental tuners, sputtering speakers, and other complaining components.

Although Mr. Bohn carries with him two large satchels containing test equipment (including a tube tester and a VOM) and replacement parts, he finds that he uses his testing equipment less often than his ear. A typical job involves ridding the setup of an annoying hum, and his task centers on locating the source of the trouble. With the "ear test," he moves connecting cable about, changes various tubes, and experiments with speaker placement.

Sometimes the job does involve more complicated effort, of course, such as aligning tuners and tracing electronic faults. After segregating and disconnecting the guilty component, he takes it along to his shop for detailed attention.

HOW TO GET STARTED

Assuming that you have a minimum stock of repair parts, tools, and equipment, you are almost ready to seek out your first patients. But prior to that you'll want to establish a rate schedule. The best system initially is to work on an hourly basis—with at least $10 the hourly rate. The minimum fee per house call, no matter how little time spent there, should be your hourly rate. Many charge more.

The figure can be adjusted upward as your enterprise becomes better known and the demand on your time increases.

Fortunately, you're not bound, in your hi-fi practice, by the medical doctor's rule against advertising. You'll not only be permitted to advertise, you must do so.

USE THESE FOUR ATTENTION-GETTERS

In addition to the usual Yellow Pages and newspaper classified ads, there are a number of other, more specialized means of calling your enterprise to the attention of people who might have need for your services.

A man in New Mexico made an arrangement with a local record store to place on its counters piles of broadsides advertising his in-home repair service.

A Maryland resident advertises regularly on a local FM radio station that features good quality music. He reasoned, and correctly so, that since most hi-fi rigs contain FM tuners, he could obtain many customers this way.

Some FM stations publish monthly program guides, and very often these guides contain advertisements. What better way to reach hi-fi fans than by inserting ads in a publication that is subscribed to only by members of the clan?

One enterprising audio repair specialist not only advertises in the monthly program guides in his area, but also has rented a list of their subscribers. He sends out literature to these subscribers about twice a year.

FIVE RELATED ENTERPRISES

Servicing the equipment is not the only way to cash in on the hi-fi and stereo boom. Here are some examples of what else is being done:

In a suburban New York county, a thriving business is based on the *installation* of home music systems. The owner of this part-time firm provides a full range of services, beginning with advice on specific equipment to fit the particular home, continuing with help in locating and purchasing it, and concluding with custom installation.

In California, a profitable enterprise has been built around antenna installation. Three FM stations are within range of the community, but each is located in a different direction. This often makes it necessary for listeners to install antenna rotators on their roofs, and not many of them are willing to handle this task themselves. With a ladder, an old panel truck, and a few tools, a business was formed. It also handles television antenna work.

A carpenter who was subject to frequent lay-offs began a spare-time high fidelity cabinet business. He does two basic kinds of work: Custom cabinetry in home situations that require built-ins, and movable cabinets designed for the specific units involved but which can be placed in just about any location.

A firm in Ohio specializes in record cabinets, the floor-to-ceiling type, and sells most of its products through the mail. Not surprisingly, many of the cabinets are sold to radio stations.

A teenager in New Jersey with a working knowledge of electronics has earned good pin money by correcting the errors of others. He works with home-built kits that for some reason failed to function when completed. Millions of kits are sold each year, and mistakes are bound to be made. He corrects the mistakes and is well paid for his efforts.

Plan 4: RESTORING TOYS

A few years ago this ad appeared in the classified section of a west coast newspaper for the first time:

> From a grandad's work-
> shop: rebuilt and repaired
> toys, including trains, dolls,
> doll carriages, tricycles, etc.
> Also, used toys bought,
> repaired. Telephone 000-
> 0000.

The response was more than Alfred Moore had expected, and within a few days practically all of his stock was sold. And he found that most of the purchasers became prospects for repair jobs on their own toys, just as many of his repair customers eventually became purchasers of items he had for sale.

Alfred Moore had thus hit upon a successful formula for a type of enterprise that is earning good money not only for him but for hundreds of others like him across the continent. The rewards, of course, are not only financial. It's the type of business that presents its owner with various other benefits, not the least of which is the knowledge that in conducting it one is bringing pleasure to numerous children.

A NEVER-ENDING SUPPLY LINE

The source of raw materials—broken toys—is practically infinite. The success of the business lies in the fact that usually it takes less time for a child to break a toy than it did for his parent to purchase it.

Scores of attics, basements, and playrooms in your own neighborhood contain all of the broken toys you need for your initial stock. Pay between 10 and 15 per cent of the original retail value and you'll earn a good profit by selling the items, after renewal, for about 50% of the original value.

Those families that have nothing to sell are prospects for repair work on items they want to keep. Thus, just about every family with youngsters is a prospect.

FOUR STEPS TO TAKE
IN LAUNCHING YOUR BUSINESS

Here's how to get your own toy hospital business under way:

1. Your initial activity should be in gaining proficiency in this type of work. It's relatively easy, but practice will be necessary in order to develop speed, and the experience you gain will enable you to estimate fees and establish prices. The best way to get this practice and experience is actually to work with some old toys. They are easily obtainable at rummage sales, second hand shops, etc.

You'll need a variety of paints, some simple tools, an assortment of nuts and bolts, sandpaper, oil, and grease.

2. When you feel confident that you've attained a reasonable degree of proficiency and that you can accomplish work rapidly enough to make it financially worthwhile, seek your first customers by inserting a small classified ad in the paper. Remember that you must confine yourself to the more expensive toys; repairing one and two dollar items is not worth the time involved.

3. Make arrangements with one or more retail stores to serve as depositories for used toys that the owners wish repaired. It's an excel-

lent source of additional business, and the 25% commission you pay to the store leaves a good profit margin for you.

4. You'll soon find that your best advertising, by far, is word of mouth. Do everything you can to encourage your customers to send their friends. If your work is good and your prices fair, they'll be happy to do so. Alfred Moore became known as "The Toy Man" in his community, a·title he welcomed because of the impact it had on his business.

WOMEN ARE NOT EXCLUDED

Men are not the only successful operators of toy hospitals. Many women are pulling in substantial spare-time incomes as well. A number of them specialize in renewing and re-clothing dolls and repairing doll houses.

Man or woman, you'll have to search far and wide to find a more satisfying venture that can be launched with so little in the way of investment or experience.

Plan 5: NON-MECHANICAL AUTOMOTIVE SERVICES

Next to its home, the costliest possession the average family has is its car (or, in many cases, "fleet" of two or more cars) and naturally most people strive to keep their autos in the best possible condition.

With car polishing serving as the base, there are many services you can provide that will meet this important need. The pay is excellent.

Polishing is the base because it's the service that attracts your customers to you. But once you've got their cars you have an opportunity to make money at a far greater profit, for the time spent, than merely polishing would provide.

HOW ONE MAN DID IT

The best example I've seen of this type of enterprise is operated by Glenn J., who entered the business several years ago. He had a two-car garage and an ample driveway, there was no limit to the city water supply, and car washing and polishing seemed to be a natural.

He inserted a small classified ad in the local newspaper saying that he would Simonize a regular-sized car for $15, a compact for $13.50, and a large luxury car for $17. These prices included, if the customer chose, free pickup and delivery. This was easily accomplished. Glenn drove his own car to the customer's home and left it while he serviced the customer's auto.

With the aid of lights, Glenn found he was able to do two cars per night. The washing was done in the driveway and the polishing inside the garage.

One evening, as he was picking up a car, he noticed a headlight had burned out. He mentioned it to the customer, who replied that he had been meaning to get a replacement but hadn't got around to it.

"You couldn't do it for me, could you?" he asked.

Glenn thought for a moment and then replied in the affirmative.

"And, by the way, there's a small scratch on the right rear fender. Think you might do something about that?" After another moment's thought, Glenn again replied in the affirmative.

A 53% HIKE IN THE BILL

Instead of a $15 polishing job, he grossed $23. The headlight (which he bought for $1.25 at an auto store on the way home) sold for $3, and he collected $5 for the scratch. Fortunately, he was familiar with an old service station standby: A touch-up can be made to match perfectly by dipping a small brush in lacquer thinner and rubbing it over some unseen area of the finish, such as under the hood. When the paint dissolves on the brush, it is applied immediately to the scratch.

The best part of it was that the work involved in installing the headlight and re-touching the scratch took less than 20 minutes. It didn't take much figuring for Glenn to realize that while his polishing work was netting him perhaps $3.50 per hour, the other work had brought $6.75 for a third of an hour—which would multiply out at better than $20 per hour! It was too good to continue to pass by.

And he didn't pass it by. Determined to capture as many of the sideline profits as possible, Glenn drew up a checklist. Whenever a car was turned over to him for polishing, he went down the list with the owner and marked the items the owner wished taken care of.

Here's the list:

- Wash
- Simonize
- Check headlights, tail lights, panel and dome lights, replacing if necessary
- Retouch minor scratches and nicks
- Charge battery
- Shampoo interior
- Rotate tires
- Change engine oil and filter
- Replace broken antenna
- Install rear radio speaker, reverberation unit, or stereo cartridge unit.

Glenn has also made a habit of giving each car a "walkaround" in the owner's presence, looking for other services it might need, and which he can perform. As a result, the average $15 polish customer actually winds up paying at least $20, with the last $5 almost clear profit.

HOW TO INCREASE THE POTENTIAL

You may discover, as Glenn did, that there's a bigger potential profit if you hire teenagers to do the polishing while you devote your time to dealing with the customers and to handling the "bonus" services they authorize.

After running a few initial ads to get your venture under way, you'll probably find that repeat business and new customers obtained by word of mouth will provide nearly all the jobs you can handle.

DON'T FORGET THIS KEY ELEMENT

A car polishing business—with sidelines—is a top-notch money-maker that can be started with just about no investment and expanded almost as much as you have the time and inclination for. The secret, of course, is to keep your eyes open for extra dollars with every job. Customers will be pleased to be able to have needed work done with no inconvenience to them, and you'll be pleased with the many added dollars you'll earn.

15 MORE REPAIR SPECIALTIES

The skills required for the following fields can be obtained through instruction courses, books, or, in some cases, through practice. None is particularly difficult to learn—and any can be the basis of a well-paying enterprise.

Piano Tuning. The piano is America's most popular instrument. With experts advising that each one be tuned at least twice a year, the call for tuners is great. Check the classified sections in any of the mechanics magazines for home study courses.

Organ Tuning. Electronic organs are becoming more popular every day. A specialist in tuning and repair has his profits cut out for him. A knowledge of electronics is required. Beyond that, a number of study books are available in this specialty, among them *Electronic Organs* published by Howard W. Sams & Co., Indianapolis.

Mending. This can be a surprisingly good money-maker for women. A lady in Kansas, for example, has some 30 families as mending "clients." For an established weekly or monthly fee, she agrees to repair and mend all of the clothing in each family as needed. It's somewhat like a clothing *insurance policy,* and as a result she's not been at a loss for work—or money.

Re-Weaving. The Fabricon Company, 1555 Howard Street, Chicago, Illinois, reports many people are making $5, $10, and even $15 for each job involving "invisible reweaving"—repairing holes and burns in clothing and fabrics. Fabricon sells a course on the subject, and free literature is available for the asking.

Bookbinding. Assignment work in making new bindings for valuable books that customers want to preserve can be most rewarding. Business is obtained by getting permission to place posters in book stores and on library bulletin boards.

Watch Repair. Once you've completed a home study course, you'll be able to undersell the downtown repair shops because of your comparatively low overhead. Get your initial business by doing repairs for your friends. If your work is good and prices low, they'll tell *their* friends, and your spare time will soon be all spoken for.

Camera Repair. Ever take a camera to a local shop for repairs, only to be told they'd have to send it away and it might take a month or two? If so, you know the need for this business. Ads in the paper and Yellow Pages stressing the quick service will bring shutterbugs flocking to your door.

Auto Radios and Stereo Units. There's money not only in repairs, but also in sales and installation. Once again, it's the speed of the work that will pay off. Auto shops usually have to send the equipment back to the factory, which can involve many weeks. Provide same-day repairs and you've got a money-maker. Sales of new equipment and installation of items customers have bought elsewhere round out the profit picture.

Typewriter Repair. Specialize in working on home machines or office models—or both. You can do cleaning and make minor adjustments "on location," and perform overhaul work in your basement shop. Do it on a per-job basis, or offer maintenance contracts. Eventually you can branch out to other office machines such as adding machines, calculators, duplicators, and photo copiers.

Lawnmowers. Just about every homeowner with a yard bigger than two feet square owns a power mower, and like anything else mechanical, these things need attention from time to time. Your services can range from sharpening to overhaul—and perhaps sales.

Sharpening. Many other things besides lawnmowers need occasional sharpening. A number of manufacturing firms that advertise in the mechanics magazines offer equipment for this along with instructions on how to build a well-paying business.

TV Repair. No one has ever taken a precise count of the thousands of men who are in business for themselves doing TV repairs, but you can bet the figure is substantial. So are the profits. And there's room for more TV repair specialists in just about every community. Naturally, it's not a stay-at-home business, because you'll be doing a lot of the minor repairs and adjustments in the homes of your customers. But you'll need a shop in your abode to handle the major work.

Bicycles. Bikes are getting fancier every day, from the spider models to the five, ten, and 15 gear jobs. It's no longer like when you and I were young and a pair of pliers would fix just about any ill. It takes a specialist. Become one and you'll have the basis of a fine business.

Locksmith. It's an ancient craft for which there still is great need. In fact, the need is probably greater now than ever, due largely to the increased crime rate. People are constantly changing and adding locks, and that's one source of business. You can be thankful that they're also losing keys with regularity. There's good money making duplicates.

Boats. The one job boating enthusiasts don't usually enjoy is preparing their craft for the water each spring. Do it for them and you'll not only enjoy their everlasting gratitude, but also a good piece of their money. It's not as seasonal as it sounds. One man I know encourages customers to deposit their boats with him when the cold weather sets in each fall; he's kept busy most of the fall, winter, and spring this way. Then in the summer he relaxes in his own boat.

7

High-Demand Used Articles You Can Sell

There's a lot of life left in tools, utensils, various kinds of equipment, playthings, and personal possessions long after their usefulness to the original owner has ended. Many of these articles are in demand by other people who can't afford or don't want to pay the "new" price or who have not been able to find anything similar in the stores.

Good money is being made by locating these items and then selling them to interested buyers. And you can have a lot of enjoyment in the process.

PROFIT FROM A BIG MARKUP SPECIALTY

There's one major advantage going for you from the first day you hang out your sign. You're not confined to the usual slim profit margin faced by most retailers. Unlike the businessman whose gross profit is 40% of what an item sells for, you'll be keeping up to 85%. In fact, there are few things you'll want to touch that won't at least give you double what you paid.

The reason for the high markup is simple. You won't be faced with rigid price schedules when you purchase, and you won't have nationally-advertised prices to compete with when you sell. The secret is to buy "cheap" and sell for what the market will bear. It may sound a bit cold but it's a fact of business life, and you are, after all, in business to make money.

HOW TO SELECT YOUR RESALE LINE

There are two criteria to follow in deciding what you are going to sell. The first concerns supply and demand. The items you choose must be available in sufficient quantity to be worthwhile, and they should be much sought-after locally.

To illustrate, let's consider antiques. Regardless of where you live, it's fairly certain that a demand exists, so half the problem is licked. But how about the supply? You can't buy from other local shops and mark up your items sufficiently to make a good profit—you'd price yourself out of business. Therefore, you'd either have to purchase the items from private owners (such as the estates of deceased persons) or you'd have to make your purchases from shops in other regions where the prices are sufficiently lower.

The second criterion is that you must have a knowledge of, and an interest in, the items being sold. How else can you judge what you're buying, and how else can you impart enthusiasm when you're selling?

That's why hobbyist-collectors usually make excellent resale businessmen. They're totally involved in their chosen field, they know it well, and they're able to use that involvement and know-how to their best financial advantage.

THE SECRET OF KEEPING CUSTOMERS COMING

Most of your customers will have the same deep interest in what you're selling as you should have, so they will not be "one-time" customers—not if you handle matters correctly. Keep them coming back year after year. That's the strategy of the top earners in the resale field!

How do you do it? Depends on what you're selling. Let's again take antiques as an example. You will, of course, keep a record of the names and addresses of all your customers, obtained from the sales slip. Periodically you can have a card printed up announcing that you have just restocked with some fine examples of . . . whatever it is that you've restocked.

Or you can keep records of the "wants" of various customers. Then, when you get something in that line, drop a note or phone them.

These techniques work for almost any resale line. The idea is to keep in regular contact with your customers. Don't depend on them to come back to you—you've got to draw them back by knowing what they're interested in and filling that want.

Plan 1: HIGH FIDELITY EXCHANGE

An interest in high fidelity is not a static thing. Those who truly enjoy it are constantly poring over magazine articles and literature concerning various components they don't presently own, but would like to.

Because of the constant introduction of new items—and the care that goes into making good high fidelity equipment—it's an expensive interest in which to indulge. Thus the need for high fidelity exchanges, "swap shops," if you will, featuring hi-fi and stereo components.

KNOW THE CUSTOMER TYPES

There are two types of people to whom you'll cater when you open your hi-fi exchange. One is the person just developing his interest, usually a young person who is not yet ready or able to buy expensive new equipment. You'll be able to offer him excellent buys in used equipment.

The other type is the person who's had an interest for some time, has had some equipment, but now wants to trade up. Frequently, he'll recognize the fact that you can offer much more for his money than can the dealer who sells new products. You'll accommodate this customer not only by filling his needs for higher grade components, but also by accepting as trade-ins the components he is replacing.

To operate this kind of business, your knowledge of the field will have to extend beyond a mere familiarity with the various types of equipment. This, of course, is vital, but since you'll have to stand behind the items you sell, a knowledge of electronics is equally necessary. It will enable you to inspect, and repair when necessary, the used items you purchase as your stock.

There are two basic methods of conducting your hi-fi resale operation. One is actually to open up a shop in your home, setting aside a room in which to display the items and receive customers. The other is to advertise and sell items on an individual basis through inexpensive *merchandise for sale* ads in the classified section of a local newspaper.

Many businesses begin with the latter method and gradually work up to the status of a regular shop.

HOW TO FIND ITEMS TO SELL

You can obtain components in the same manner, and just as easily, as you sell them—through the classifieds. A typical ad might read:

> Wanted: Used high fidelity components. Amplifiers, tuners, recorders, tape decks, turntables, etc. Reasonably priced.

A rule of thumb is to pay no more than 25% of the original retail price for any item, and preferably less. This will allow you a markup of at least 100%, because your selling price will generally be half of the original selling price. In making purchases you'll discount even further, of course, if the merchandise has to be repaired or overhauled.

In selling your items, it is usually best to advertise one specific component as an attention-getter, followed either by a listing of other items you have for sale, or a general statement that you feature all types of components.

For example, this ad might run under *merchandise for sale:*

> Fisher stereo tuner, Model FM-100-B, reconditioned, $85. Also various other stereo components all in excellent condition. Phone 000-0000.

You'll get a number of calls from people who are not interested in the tuner, but will ask, "By any chance do you have a . . ." and thus you'll make a lot more sales than if you were to omit the part about "various other stereo components."

HOW TO OPEN A SHOP

The same type of advertising that is used for individual items will bring people to a full-fledged shop, located in your basement, game room, or garage—but when they arrive they'll be greeted by an array of other equipment on display. This leads to what the big merchants like to call "impulse buying." A person who came to buy a $90 tuner may leave poorer by, say, $175 because of the tape deck he also purchased.

Have some stickers printed, giving your name, address, and phone number, and be sure that no equipment goes out of your shop without one attached. Then, when the customer is in the market for something else in the future, he'll think of you first.

It's best to offer some sort of guarantee on what you sell. Thirty days unconditional should be sufficient. A customer's natural hesitancy to purchase used equipment will be broken if he knows you stand behind what you sell.

AN IMPORTANT TIP

Subscribe to, and file permanently, the major high fidelity magazines. Reading the current issues will keep you abreast of new equipment and trends, and having back issues on file will enable you to look up equipment that is no longer made and ascertain its original selling price as well as what the testing labs had to say about it.

WHAT'S THE PROFIT POTENTIAL?

It depends, of course, on your volume, but by selling just two average items per week you should be able to clear $75. You can build up a trade that gives you a fairly consistent profit of double that or more, depending on your available time and the population of the area from which your customers are drawn.

Plan 2: CHILDREN'S CLOTHING

What's one of the biggest expenses for a family with growing children? After the mortgage and food, it is probably clothing. Children outgrow it so rapidly that soon after a child is completely outfitted in new apparel he needs a wardrobe several sizes larger.

This means that a lot of children's clothing is actually worn much less than would be a similar piece of adult apparel.

This "short use" of children's clothing can be the keystone of a home-based business for you. Two factors make it possible:

1. Due to the short period of service the average piece of clothing receives, it usually remains in good condition when it becomes of no further use to the child for whom it was purchased.

2. Because of the constant need to keep their children in clothing of the proper size, many parents welcome the opportunity to obtain good used clothing at bargain prices.

You can supply the clothing and you can offer the bargain prices. You're about to learn where you can obtain it at a sufficiently low price so that an ample profit can be made, and you'll learn how to sell this clothing by reaching the people who can use it most.

YOUR BEST SOURCE OF SUPPLY

The best source for good used clothing at prices which will allow a profit is the rummage sale. Church groups and other nonprofit and charitable organizations regularly hold rummage sales in order to raise funds. Some groups conduct their sales two and three times per year, and there is no area of the country where, all told, dozens of rummage sales aren't held annually.

Members and friends of the sponsoring groups donate their outgrown or unwanted clothing, enabling the group to offer it for sale at extremely low prices. A selective buyer can wind up with some tremendous bargains at every sale he attends.

You may wonder how an individual can purchase clothing at a rummage sale and resell it to others at a profit when all the person who seeks such clothing need do is go to the rummage sale himself. The answer is this: While many people do not hesitate to purchase good used clothing, they often are not overly anxious to let the world know they are doing it. One is apt to be seen by many people at a rummage sale, and while there is nothing wrong with purchasing used clothing, there are those who might tend to be embarrassed.

You, on the other hand, will be selling from the privacy of your home to one customer at a time. No one need be embarrassed. Another reason is the fact that a mother would have to attend a lot of sales in order to outfit her children, while she can obtain a broad selection by making one stop at your home.

ENJOY A GOOD MARKUP

You should aim for a markup of at least 300%. If a girl's dress costs you 50¢ at a sale, the minimum price to set for it is $1.50.

Not all the clothing you purchase will be in perfect condition. Sometimes particularly low prices are placed on items lacking a button, having a drooping hem, etc. A few minutes with needle and thread once you get the items home can more than pay for themselves.

Bearing in mind the 300% minimum markup, you will probably set prices in this range:

GIRLS' CLOTHING	BOYS' CLOTHING
Dresses $1.25–$1.75	Shirts 35¢–50¢
Sweaters 60¢–75¢	Sweaters 60¢–75¢
Blouses 35¢–50¢	Coats $2.50–$3.50
Coats $2.50–$3.50	Suits $2–$4
Suits $1.50–$1.75	Dress Trousers $1.25–$1.75 (Boys' everyday trousers will be unavailable, as they are worn out too rapidly.)

ATTRACTING BUSINESS

Your customers will be obtained through classified ads you have inserted in your local paper. Your ad might read something like this:

Good used children's clothing, various sizes. Outgrown by their original owners, but still plenty of wear left.

When people call (and you'll probably be surprised at how many do) set up definite appointments with each. This way you will not have more than one buyer examining clothing at a time, and you'll be able to devote full attention to each customer.

Another advantage of the appointment system is that by knowing who is coming and when, you can display to best advantage the type of clothing in which that particular customer is interested. For instance, if a mother calls about clothing for a five-year-old girl, you can lay out all appropriate garments, leaving the rest of your selection closeted. No fancy display arrangements will be needed; the items can be laid out on a couch, bed, chairs, and/or tables.

HOW ELLA THOMAS DID IT

Ella Thomas got into the used clothing business with items that had been outgrown by her own daughter. A classified ad brought her a wave of customers who purchased $200 worth of clothing in a week's time. Overwhelmed by how well the items had sold, Mrs. Thomas experimented by purchasing some additional items at her church's rummage sale and offering them for sale. Needless to say, the experiment paid off.

This launched her business. She's found that she is most successful by concentrating on three periods of the year. The best time to sell is late summer and early fall, when school reconvenes; spring is second; and good results are also obtained in mid-winter.

Mrs. Thomas is not putting a great deal of effort into her business. It remains largely in the hobby category, but nevertheless clears about $2,000 per year. Mrs. Thomas feels confident that, if she chose, she could easily double that figure.

Plan 3: RELICS OF BYGONE DAYS

Some people are satisfied with reproductions of early Americana in their homes; others crave the real thing. There is a tremendous market for utensils, tools, and other items used by families in the early days of our country. They are employed today not in their original utilitarian uses, but as decorative pieces to make modern-day homes and properties more attractive.

An excellent income can be derived from locating and selling such items—and doing it is much simpler than you might think.

One couple I have in mind has drawn steady profits from this type of business over a number of years. It began when Warren Ruggles purchased two old wagon wheels at a country auction while in Vermont. He paid four dollars with the intent of painting them and then installing them at the head of his driveway as markers.

His plan went awry, however, soon after he arrived back at his suburban home and spotted a classified ad in the local newspaper, offering wagon wheels at $17.50 per pair. He realized that if he could sell *his* for that much, the profit would be greater than 400%. He did, it was, and a business was born.

Warren decided to return to Vermont another weekend to purchase all the wagon wheels he could locate. Prior to his trip he inserted a small classified ad in several Vermont newspapers offering to buy such wheels and asking prospective sellers to drop him a line. There were four replies. One farmer had eight for sale, another person ten, another two, and the fourth had four.

After some bargaining at each stop, Mr. and Mrs. Ruggles managed to get the wheels for an average price of about two dollars each, a total of $50 for all 24. And at one of the stops they picked up an old parlor organ—the kind you pump with your feet—for $30, on speculation.

Two days later, this ad appeared in the paper:

> Old wagon wheels, $17.50
> pair. Also old parlor organ
> in good playing condition,
> $100.

It seemed that the phone never stopped ringing. Within three days the organ and all of the wheels had been sold at the advertised prices—a total of $310, and a gross profit of $230. Not bad for an enjoyable weekend!

Their success caused Warren Ruggles and his wife to reason that if wagon wheels and organs would sell at such a good profit, why not other items that might be desirable in gracing local homes? It seemed clear that if Mr. and Mrs. Ruggles could continue to obtain these items, there would be a ready market for them.

So they went at their project on a bigger scale, running regular ads in the rural newspaper seeking wagon wheels, parlor organs, old farm utensils, buggies, commodes, etc. One weekend a month they drove to Vermont to pick up merchandise, pulling a two-wheel trailer Warren had bought. A corner of their basement was cleared for storage and display.

The first year, the Ruggles cleared $3,500 on their part-time enterprise, and profits have increased each year since.

HOW YOU CAN PROFIT

This kind of business is by no means limited to someone who can travel to Vermont. Your only requirements concerning locale are these:

1. Your home should be in a heavily developed area where there are few, if any, farms where old items can be bought locally.
2. Within driving range there should be a rural section that is a good source of supply.

Finding your supply may take some travelling about and involve a bit of research, but the effort will be well worthwhile. Actually, there are few residential areas in the country not within easy driving range of rural sections that are potential supply sources. Warren, for example, lives near New York City, the largest metropolis in the nation.

As Mrs. Ruggles explains, one of the greatest advantages of the business is that you don't have to know anything about antiques. "We merely buy items found in old attics and barns, items usually of a rough or crude nature. Condition is unimportant, since most buyers enjoy restoring and painting them."

To help the readers of this book, Warren Ruggles compiled a list of items that sell readily. After each item are two figures; the first is the average purchase price, and the second the average selling price. Prices often vary due to condition.

Wagon wheels $4 pr.; $17.50

Sap buckets $1; $4

Clocks $20; $45

Oil lamps $4; $10

Barn lanterns $1; $3

Old picture frames 300% markup

Commodes $15; $35

Chamber dishes $2; $5

Wash bowl & pitcher $10; $25

Buggies $30; $120

Sleighs (horse-drawn) $20; $75

Neck yokes 10¢; $1.50

Whiffle trees 25¢; $3

Crude tools 400% markup

Sleighbell sets $12; $25

Flat irons $1; $3

Grain boxes 50¢; $3.50

Old wooden boxes 500% markup

Old calendars 10¢; $1.25

Jugs $1; $3

Bean pots $1; $2.50

Parlor organs $30; $100

Horse collars, other harness parts $1; $4

Ox yokes $10; $30

Spinning wheels $10; $27.50

Flax wheels $30; $50

Stools 50¢; $3.50

Bread mixers $2.50; $8

Butter workers $5; $15

Cobblers' work benches $10; $25

Little school bells $3; $7.50

School desks $1; $5

Blanket chests $10; $30

Wood or coal-burning stoves $12.50; $30

Kitchen sink pumps $3; $7

"The people from whom we buy these things don't realize the tremendous market that exists for them," Warren comments. It has not been rare for him to buy a box of odds and ends for a dollar and sell the contents individually for as much as $15.

What is junk to one person can be treasure to another.

Plan 4: BOOKS

The value of a hard cover book continues long after its initial owner has finished reading it. The value to *him* may be gone, but the book is still of considerable interest to others who would like to read it.

By serving as the go-between—buying books that others are done with and selling to those who seek good volumes at bargain prices—you can develop a lucrative spare-time business. Many people are doing it.

How much do used books sell for? Many home-based shops charge an average price of 50¢ per volume. They are generally purchased by the dealer for a maximum of 25¢ each. The rule-of-thumb is to charge at least twice what you paid.

HOW TO OBTAIN GOOD USED BOOKS

The only efficient and economical way to purchase your books (except when they are brought in to your shop) is to buy in bulk lots. You cannot afford to travel to someone's home to examine and purchase as few as ten volumes. Fifty books should be the minimum grouping you seek on any purchase trip, no matter how near to your home.

You'll receive many leads by inserting small ads in the "Merchandise Wanted" columns of your local paper, and under "Books, Used, Bought & Sold" in the Yellow Pages. You can also obtain books within your price range by patronizing the book sales sponsored as fund-raising affairs by libraries, churches, and other non-profit groups.

After your shop is open and has become well known, people will bring volumes in to you—and in such cases you can afford to buy in small lots. Some dealers even have an arrangement in which they trade one book for two volumes turned in.

ORGANIZE YOUR STOCK

After you've obtained a fair supply (several thousand volumes to start) you are ready to get organized. Set aside one room for the purpose (it can even be your garage if it is well lighted) and arrange the books on shelves, tables, or long benches.

It is important to organize your stock by category (fiction, gardening, music, history, etc.). You'll sell many more this way. People soon tire of looking through random groupings and may never see a number of books that would interest them.

HOW TO DRAW CUSTOMERS

A running classified or small display ad in a local newspaper will draw many customers, as will use of the Yellow Pages. A sign out front will attract the curious and serve as an identifier for those who seek out your shop for the first time.

It will probably be necessary to be open during evening hours, and because of this it would be advisable to list the hours in your ads and on your sign.

If you sell only 200 books per week in your spare time, you can net about $40; increasing the volume by upping the hours you are open and doing more advertising can increase the net substantially.

Plan 5: COMMISSION SALES OF HANDIWORK, ART

A fascinating way to make money at home, meet a lot of interesting people, and at the same time provide a genuinely useful service is to use one or more rooms of your home as a showplace for the handiwork of others. Thousands of people have hobbies that involve the making of useful, decorative, or tasty items—but have no way to dispose of these items profitably.

Your home can serve as the basis of an enterprise in which these items are sold to the public on a commission basis. On display and offered for sale can be handmade articles, art (including paintings, drawings, and sculpture), beaded rugs, knit goods, crocheted pieces, home-canned foods, candy, weaved items . . . the list is practically endless.

The advantage of using a home for this type of enterprise is the fact that it *is* a home. The surroundings do away with the aura of commercialism, remind customers that these aren't machine-made or mass-produced products, and make the individual items more attractive and therefore more salable.

The average commission paid to those who conduct such arts-and-crafts enterprises is 25%. Because the items remain the property of the maker until they are sold, you have no merchandise investment to be concerned about.

HOW TO OBTAIN CONSIGNORS

The easiest way to attract your initial consignments is to get in touch with senior citizens associations, church and service groups, 4-H clubs, and other organizations whose members are likely to be involved in the arts and crafts field, food preserving, etc. Small advertisements in the local press announcing your service should also prove fruitful.

One person with a home-based arts and crafts center makes a practice of reading all of the local newspapers regularly with an eye toward feature articles on hobbyists involved in making items that might be salable. Each hobbyist is contacted by mail or telephone and invited to consign. This dealer also checks the classified ads and gets in touch with advertisers who seem to be likely prospects.

HOW TO OBTAIN CUSTOMERS

First of all, each person who brings items to you to be sold will automatically be exposed to the *other* items you have for sale. You'll find that most consignors are easily converted into customers.

If you live in an area that attracts tourists, get in touch with the chamber of commerce, tourist bureau, or information center—and the hotel and resort managers—and ask them to let visitors know you have on display samples of the handiwork of local residents. Tourists are usually anxious to obtain such items as memorabilia of their journey.

Develop a mailing list, with the names drawn from your consignors, customers, and others interested in homemade articles. Every few months an inexpensive mimeographed brochure can be sent out listing some of the latest items to be offered.

If your home is on a main road or highway, a sign out front will attract passersby and, in fact, will probably be your principal means of advertising.

POINTERS ON CONDUCTING YOUR BUSINESS

Whenever possible, display the items in a manner as close as possible to what would be their normal setting. Paintings and drawings, for example, should actually be hung on walls rather than laid out on tables or left on the floor leaning against the wall.

Encourage your consignors to set reasonable prices. If an item is over-priced, chances are it won't sell; therefore it will be taking up valuable space without providing any income.

Always keep complete records, which begin from the time an item is consigned and continue to the time it is sold. It's too easy to forget who consigned what several months ago. And when an item is sold, report promptly to the consignor.

One way to increase the volume of your business is to allow use of one of your rooms for arts and crafts courses and demonstrations. This brings people interested in the field into your home, exposing them to your merchandise.

HOW TWO PEOPLE DID IT

Mary Fredericks used practically her entire house as a display area, giving customers the grand tour. They found attractive items in the living room, dining area, kitchen, bedrooms—even the bathroom. Since so much of her home was made available for display, there was no cluttering of merchandise and most items looked as if they were meant to be there. The surroundings helped make many sales.

Cary Barkson uses just one room for displaying merchandise. It's a former recreation room that has an outside entrance. Since he now is retired from his job, he's home much of the time, available to welcome customers and consignors. In addition to the arts and crafts work that is consigned, he offers foodstuffs prepared by Mrs. Barkson.

This type of business offers plenty of opportunity for expansion. A number of ventures that began part-time in the home have since expanded to become full-fledged arts and crafts shops, either attached to the home or on separate premises.

13 MORE RESALE SHOP SPECIALTIES

Thrift Shop. Good, serviceable clothing for adults finds a ready market. You can operate as a regular shop or advertise a few pieces at a time. See the earlier section on children's clothing for tips on how to obtain and sell your items.

Art Exchange. Housewives frequently tire of the paintings on their walls and, when given the opportunity, are pleased at being able to "trade them in" on other paintings. This will keep you steadily supplied with both paintings and profits. The usual price range for the type of work handled in an art exchange is $25–$250.

Business Machines. Typewriters, adders, calculators, duplicators, copiers, addressers—there's a need for some or all of these in most offices, and many firms, especially the smaller ones, are satisfied with used equipment. Don't forget rentals, as some companies prefer to rent rather than buy.

Antique Car Parts. A hobby that is growing in popularity is the restoration of old cars. Search old garages and barns and you can find some badly needed parts for these hobbyists. One way to sell (and buy on occasion, too) is to attend the "flea markets" designed expressly for antique car buffs.

Camera Exchange. See the first plan in this chapter. Obtaining and selling used cameras can be done in much the same manner as conducting a hi-fi exchange. The market is equally large, and many individuals have found it to be an excellent basis for a lucrative enterprise.

LP Albums. In recent years, a number of businesses featuring used phonograph albums have sprung up, many of them operated from homes. Selling LPs is not unlike selling books; see Plan 4.

Magazines. Back-copy magazines—particularly those of a lasting appeal such as the scientific, historic, or geographical—are always in demand. If you live in a heavily-populated area, a good dollar-volume can be developed by dealing in these publications.

Bicycles. Young families can't always afford to purchase new bikes for each of the children. They often seek to buy good used ones instead.

Autos. Yes, autos . . . provided you deal in them one or two at a time. Regular dealers usually take in more older models on trade than they can handle, and they make the surplus available to wholesalers. You can often purchase these cars at the wholesale price, but they'll be "as is." Re-condition them yourself and sell them privately, and you've got the basis for a good spare-time income. A modern-day version of the old horse trader.

Baby Supplies. When baby outgrows his crib, playpen, carriage, stroller, and high chair, Mom and Pop are usually more than glad to sell them at rock bottom prices. Then when some other family experiences a blessed event, they're generally more than glad to pay you a somewhat higher price. That's the way money is made.

Musical Instruments. Accordions, violins, guitars, amplifiers—these are some of the instruments for which there is a considerable demand on the used market. You don't have to know how to play them in order to sell them . . . purchasers do their own "demonstrating."

Firearms. The real money is in the antique items, but modern equipment sells well, too. A state, county, or city license will probably be required.

Antique Shop. Once you've obtained your stock, all you'll probably have to do to get started is hang out a shingle. Very few antique shops do much advertising. And what if there *are* a dozen other shops nearby? They're making money or they wouldn't be there. One advantage of dealing in antiques is that as your stock lies on the shelf it is slowly but surely increasing in value . . . something few other businesses can claim.

8

How to Put Your
Home to Work for You

A home can be much more than mere shelter for your spare-time earnings project. It can be the *basis* of that project. The available space in your home—be it one room or five—can produce income in and of itself. You're about to learn how.

SELECT A WELL-PAYING
HOSPITALITY PROJECT

All of the plans in this chapter stem from one central theme: Allowing others the use of part of your home. There are so many ways in which you can do this—so many widely varied profit opportunities—that you should have no difficulty in choosing one to match your home and circumstances.

Your role will be that of a host or hostess, welcoming others who pay well for the use of the facilities you offer—be it space for meetings or club projects, lodging for overnight guests, or any of the other hospitality projects outlined here. As you'll discover, some of them are highly unique. Their originators developed these enterpises through trial and error until they reached the desired point of profitability. You'll benefit from all of this by following the specialized techniques that have made each plan an outstanding success.

LEARN THE VALUE OF YOUR EXTRA SPACE

You may find that considering a hospitality project requires some changes in your pattern of thinking about a home business. Up until now you have concentrated on work projects that, for the most part can be carried out alone at home. Customers might come and go, but only to transact business, and this involves a few moments at the most.

But hospitality projects actually open part of your home to the public, and this takes some getting used to. Your paying customers may be spending hours at a time in your "business space" . . . or they may even live there. The big benefit, of course, is the fact that much more money can usually be earned, for time spent, than in most other types of home business.

HOW TO MATCH THE PLAN
WITH YOUR HOME OR APARTMENT

The representative plans included here feature varying space requirements, ranging from part of one room to all of several rooms. Naturally, your first consideration will be the amount of space you have to devote and how that space meets the requirements of each plan.

But using your home for profit requires more than the physical structure. *You* have to be in it. These are, after all, hospitality projects. Thus the plan not only has to fit your home, it has to fit *you*. It has to be something you enjoy doing.

It's also important to consider the nature of the community in which you live. The success of your business will depend on how well you can adapt your available space to the needs of that community. Is it a "new" town with a predominance of young residents? Pick a plan that caters to them. Is your home in or near a commercial or office district? Then choose a plan that serves business enterprises.

What it boils down to, therefore, is that there are three basic considerations in choosing a hospitality project:

1. Your available space
2. Your interests
3. Your community

Keep these criteria in mind as you study the plans that follow.

Plan 1: LODGING

A woman in Maryland who was faced with the problem of having to support herself when her husband died a number of years ago found the solution within the four walls of her large home. She had been debating whether or not to take a job in her community, and had been thinking how fortunate she was to live in a location that put her close to a wide array of employment opportunities.

Suddenly it came to her that if the location was convenient for her, it would be convenient for others as well. And she had plenty of spare rooms . . .

Today, Adelaide Reynolds lives comfortably on the income her home provides. With minor alterations, her house was made capable of taking in five roomers. In addition, two apartments are rented, one on the first floor and another, a studio affair, in the attic.

SELECT YOUR OWN OPPORTUNITY

There are a number of ways in which lodging facilities in *your* home can bring in cash, and you can do it on any scale you choose. Here are the four basic categories:

1. Rooming house
2. Boarding house
3. Tourist home
4. Apartments

IT'S EASY TO RUN A ROOMING HOUSE

Renting rooms is the easiest of the four. The only requirements are simple furnishings in each room, regular changes of linen, and convenient access to a bathroom. Most rooming houses are located near the center of busy towns or in industrial neighborhoods.

MAKE MEALS YOUR DRAWING CARD

Running a boarding house can be a pleasant activity if you don't mind having a crowd for supper every night. Your prices, of course, will be higher than if meals were not included, but don't expect to make a fortune on the food. Your basic profit will come from the part of the rent that covers the living quarters; food service will do little more than pay its own way. It does, however, act as an important drawing card.

TOURIST HOME PROS AND CONS

Taking in overnight guests has the drawback of providing income on a somewhat less steady basis, but the advantage of offering bigger profits per night/per room. Since most of your guests are tourists, their stays are generally confined to only a night or two, and they pay much higher rates than they would on a monthly basis. Tourist homes do well on major highways (provided they are located in attractive settings), in towns offering good vacation facilities, and in areas popular with outdoor enthusiasts.

A couple in Vermont, for example, bought an old home in a location that qualifies on all three points. Nestled in an attractive setting alongside a major highway in a resort area, it is also near well known hunting and skiing locations. Tourists fill the guest rooms during the summer; hunters in the fall; skiers in the winter.

STABLE INCOME FROM APARTMENTS

Renting apartments can involve a larger initial investment, but the conversion cost is offset by the more stable income. People who live in apartments, particularly unfurnished ones, are apt to remain much longer than roomers or boarders; it is not as easy for an apartment dweller to move out as it is for a person who need only pack a bag. Once again, location is of prime importance. The closer you are to commercial, industrial, and recreational centers, the more likely you are to keep your units rented—and at higher rates.

CHECK THE LEGAL REQUIREMENTS

After determining which of the categories is for you, the next step is to ascertain what state or local laws might affect your operation. In large cities, for instance, rooming and boarding houses require licenses and they are regularly inspected. Safety and sanitation codes are rigidly enforced.

In many areas, zoning ordinances and building codes may affect conversion of a home into apartments, so these must be checked.

The amount you charge for your rooms, boarding privileges, or apartments will depend upon local conditions. Check the rates in comparable lodgings in your community, and use them as your guide. In a tourist home, the rates will probably vary from season to season.

If your neighborhood has sufficient need for the type of lodging facility you've chosen (and if it doesn't, you've made a wrong choice) you'll have no difficulty attracting tenants. Often a sign in the window or a shingle out front, perhaps supplemented by a small three-liner in the newspaper, are all that's required to fill vacancies.

If you have apartments and don't mind paying a commission, you can enlist the aid of real estate brokers.

Plan 2: PET HOSTELRY

There are many people who don't like putting their pets in a kennel when they go on vacation or business trips. While most kennels are large, clean, and well run, they don't provide the individual care that these pet owners wish for their animals.

That's why excellent profits are being made by those who take in household pets as "paying guests." Their businesses thrive because they provide individualized care in accordance with what is specified by each owner. This includes adherence to special menus, administration of any medication that is prescribed, a good brushing of dogs once each day, and providing each canine or feline guest with two exercise walks daily. At other times they enjoy ample pens or cages.

A BUSINESS FOR EVERY LOCATION

A pet hostelry can be successfully operated just about anywhere—from a large farmyard to a small apartment in the city. The only difference is in the type and scale. If you live in the country and have spacious grounds, you'll be able to accommodate all pets. If your home is in a densely populated area, the number of dogs you can keep will be limited by the local zoning regulations and the tolerance of your neighbors to barking, but you should have little difficulty in dealing with the various other pets, including cats, caged birds, goldfish, even rabbits and hamsters.

Should your home be a small apartment, it is still possible, as you will learn, to draw a spare-time income caring for winged and finned creatures.

Because of the specialized care involved in operating a pet hostelry, the rates are higher than those of a kennel. Large dogs, for example, bring in $4–$5 per day, smaller canines $3–$4, and cats proportionately less.

HOW TO LAUNCH A FULL-SCALE HOSTELRY

Begin by setting up two or three runs several feet wide and at least ten feet in length. This size would equal or be better than what the average kennel has to offer.

You can obtain customers by sending notices to local pet stores, dog clubs, and to names on the pet owners list maintained by the municipal clerk who collects dog license fees. A Yellow Pages ad would also help.

Your advertising should stress the individual care you provide; this, after all, is what sets you apart from your competition. Let your customers know their pets will be treated exactly in accordance with their instructions and just as if they were doing it themselves, and you'll find them more than willing to pay the prices you have established.

If you live in a closely-knit residential neighborhood, you may have to turn your attention to caring for smaller pets. If you handle dogs at all, only one or two can be kept at a time because of the noise and potential nuisance factor. Chances are, though, that cats will be the largest animals you can accept. Provide them with a good play area in a heated basement or garage, make sure it's escape proof, give them a sandbox toilet area, and you're in business.

Tending to birds and tropical fish is even easier. The instructions you'll receive from each owner, perhaps supplemented by a reference book or two, will provide you with sufficient knowledge to handle the tasks successfully.

HOW OTHERS HAVE DONE IT

Everly Haskins lives in a suburban community on the west coast. He recognized the need for a pet hostelry when his own dog lost ten pounds during a stay at a local kennel. He attributed it to lack of individual care.

"It was an obvious assumption," he explains, "that if my dog got no special treatment, neither did other people's dogs. So, I decided to do something about it. I set up some pens in my basement, running its full length, and began taking in boarders—vowing to treat each one as if it were my own."

The basement is 33 feet long, so each of the pens provides plenty of exercise room. The noise problem doesn't amount to much because the dogs are inside. Everly gives the dogs outside exercise by walking them twice daily, either singly or in pairs.

His limit is three dogs at any given time, but his basement rarely has an empty pen.

"People now make reservations at least two weeks ahead of time. I get $4.50 per dog regardless of size, which means I receive $13.50 for what adds up to about an hour's work daily plus food."

In her city apartment, Madge Vester is not able to harbor dogs or cats. But she does accept a stream of visitors from the bird and fish world. Her contacts with pet shops have provided most of her business. Miss Vester houses her enterprise in a spare room in which are installed a number of small tanks and bird cages; usually, however, the customers bring their own tanks and cages.

Since these creatures take up very little space, Miss Vester rarely has to turn down business due to a "full house." Her rates vary according to the amount and type of food used, but her enterprise can be counted on to bring in at least $35 per week. With hardly any work involved, it's a business that she finds both pleasant and rewarding.

There are numerous expansion possibilities in the pet hostelry field. Those who harbor dogs can take up breeding and sell registered pups; obedience training is another possibility. Similarly, those who are restricted to the smaller creatures can increase their incomes by breeding fish.

Plan 3: DAY NURSERY

Why not capitalize on kids?

You can do it by performing a valuable service that will be appreciated by many grateful mothers. In your own home with very little investment you can open a day nursery, caring for youngsters between two and six years of age.

Working mothers will send their tots to you on a Monday-through-

Friday basis, and numerous others will be happy to know of a place where they can drop off their youngsters while they make shopping trips or attend club meetings.

The average rate for child care on a five day per week basis is $20; for a single day it's $5. For this, you provide a hot meal and perhaps a snack plus constant supervision.

THE ESSENTIALS FOR SUCCESS

Your most important requirement will be a love of children. Have you had experience caring for a number of them at a time? Did you enjoy it? Then the chances are you have the temperament required for a day nursery.

As for physical facilities, the prime necessity will be adequate space inside your home. This can be one large room to serve as the main play area, or several smaller ones (although it's much easier to keep your eye on youngsters when they're together in the same room). You should also have ground floor toilet facilities and adequate closet space for storage of outer clothing and playthings.

You'll need a good-sized yard, preferably to the rear of your home or otherwise inaccessible to the street. Fencing it in would help. During warm weather periods the children will be out-of-doors as much as possible, and every precaution must be taken to assure their safety.

Your home should be centrally located in a fair-sized community so that there will be a nucleus of young families nearby from which to draw your business.

You'll have to stock up on items to keep your children occupied and happy. Included will be appropriate games, blocks, toys, dolls, books, and perhaps a television set. In the yard, swings and slides will be needed. The investment for these items should not amount to more than a few hundred dollars.

HOW TO ATTRACT BUSINESS

The old standbys—classifieds in the paper and in the Yellow Pages—will give you a good start. Other steps, if needed, include contacting schools and large places of employment. Mothers looking for a nursery often inquire at schools and where they work.

Once you have become established, there will be little effort required to keep your nursery filled to the capacity you have set. After your initial advertising, most of your new youngsters will be sent to you as the result of word passed on by parents who have been satisfied with your service.

Experience will show you how large your capacity should be. You might start by setting half a dozen as the limit, and then gradually raise it as your efficiency and knowledge of the operation increase. Some women have been able to accommodate as many as 15 children without having to hire helpers.

But even if your limit is ten, your weekly gross will be $200, and between $125 and $150 of that amount will be profit.

SOME TIPS FROM MARILYN GANTER

Marilyn Ganter has operated a day nursery for a number of years, and she offers these bits of advice gleaned from her experience:

• In addition to obtaining the full name, address, and phone number of every mother who brings a child to you, be sure to get an emergency number—somewhere to call if the mother is not at home. This might be her place of employment, her husband's office number, or the number of a close relative or friend.

• When a child is brought to you for the first time, fill out a simple "registration" form that will include information on special dietary requirements, any pertinent health condition, and personality traits that need watching—such as a tendency to wander away.

• Don't forget to check with your insurance agent and/or lawyer on the types of insurance you'll need to protect you from financial liability in the event of accidents, illnesses, etc. Also check to determine if there are any local license requirements.

• There will, upon occasion, be circumstances involving problem children who defy all attempts to have them conform. When you have made every reasonable effort to correct the situation, but without success, notify the mother that the child is not welcome. You are running a day nursery, not a reform school.

Despite the occasional problems, Marilyn Ganter says, "A day nursery can be a wonderful and exciting way to earn a good income at home."

Launching a nursery was a decision Marilyn made after debating whether or not to return to a job she had once held. "I'm happier than ever that I didn't return to my old job. This is more fun—and it pays better, too."

Plan 4: HOBBY CENTER

The do-it-yourself boom continues at full blast, and wherever there's a boom there are profits. Here's a unique way in which you can partake of some of them.

The plan is best introduced by recounting the story of Elton Canzi, whose well-equipped woodworking shop was the envy of his friends. So much so that there was always somebody asking to use it. It got to the point where his wife jokingly suggested that he charge for its use by the hour.

Well, why not? Perhaps woodworking enthusiasts *would* be willing to pay for the use of equipment that would cost them hundreds of dollars if they had to go out and buy it.

Naturally, when you've been providing your friends with a privilege free of charge, it can be a bit awkward suddenly to impose a fee. So Elton decided to put a small test ad in the paper to see how the idea would go over with strangers. It read:

> Hobbyists—Use my wood-
> working shop, completely
> outfitted with power tools,
> $1.25 per hour. Tel. 000-
> 0000.

He also sent cards to teachers of adult ed courses in woodworking, and to high school manual arts teachers.

The response was surprisingly good, and before long the machines in the basement were running all weekend and most evenings. Elton found he could fit three or four persons in simultaneously, since there was rarely a conflict in which two persons wanted to use the same piece of equipment at the same time.

They say that success breeds success, and Elton's story proves it. The first expansion step came after he noted that people were continually seeking to "borrow" nails, screws, and wood. He put in a complete line of such items—for sale.

The shop soon got so busy that it reminded Elton of the arts and crafts center *he* had used at Fort Bliss during his Army days. Soldiers had flocked to the center during their off-duty hours to use its various facilities: the woodworking shop, the darkroom, the auto repair station, etc.

ANOTHER EXPANSION STEP

And thinking of the arts and crafts center gave Elton another idea. Why not add a darkroom? Amateur photographers would probably be more than happy to pay for the privilege of using it. So he built one in the corner of the basement through which the water pipes traveled.

His expectations were correct. The darkroom caught on as rapidly as the workshop had—despite the higher fee of $2 per hour. This was necessitated by the fact that only one person could use it at a time. A sideline source of profit was the sale of paper and chemicals.

Elton recognized a good thing when he saw it. And why not make a good thing even better? Once again returning in memory to his Army days, he recalled the popularity of the auto repair shop. It provided the men an opportunity to work on their own cars with tools and facilities on a par with what service stations used.

Elton spent a weekend digging a repair pit in his rear yard, and he invested in some top-grade mechanic's tools. He also put in a supply of motor oil, filters, spark plugs, and other common parts and accessories. This phase of the enterprise met with success equal to those that had preceded it.

It goes without saying that Elton is making good money in his enterprise. It does require someone to be at home at all times, but with Elton, his wife, and his children, this has not proven to be a problem.

Most people would not choose to conduct a home business on as elaborate a scale as that of Elton Canzi. The point is that just one of these ventures can provide a fine financial return.

CHOOSE FROM MANY OTHER PLANS

You need not be confined to the services outlined in Elton's story. There are numerous other do-it-yourself fields from which you can draw your clientele.

Here are some, as taken from my files:

In Arkansas, a printing hobbyist lost interest in that pursuit, and his press, along with a large supply of type, lay unused in the basement. A few small ads in the paper brought a number of prospects interested in using the equipment. His average net is between $20 and $25 per week—much more than he cleared with the small printing jobs he had formerly undertaken.

An artist in a large eastern city had a perfect sky-lit studio, and wondered if other artists would like to make use of it. He found they did and that they were willing to pay well.

In another city, a fortunate gentleman who has some land to the rear of his home has afforded apartment dwellers an opportunity to have their own gardens. He leases out small plots, and for an added fee will even keep the garden weeded!

In a southern community, a young man with a keen interest in electronics has a well-equipped shop that is available for other hobbyists to use at a fee.

The list could go on and on, but the point is made. Other people will pay to use your hobby equipment and facilities. The opportunities in this field are limited only by your own imagination and ingenuity.

Plan 5: REST HOME

Despite the high cost of staying in a nursing home, thousands of people who really don't need that kind of care do it because there is no other place to go.

Such is the plight of the person who has been released from the hospital following an operation—a person whose need for medical treatment has ended but who has not gained sufficient strength to care for himself in his own home, and has no one to care for him.

Or take the case of the senior citizen who is in good health but too advanced in years to be able to live alone.

Or the person overcome by fatigue who needs a period of complete rest "to get away from it all."

These circumstances are common. These are people who don't need nursing care, but who do need a certain amount of attention.

And that's where you can come in. Without any special training you can operate a rest home—in a category somewhere between a boarding house and a nursing home—and enjoy the excellent income this type of facility provides.

The requirements for space and time are higher than in many other businesses, but so are the rewards. Let's take a look.

HOW TO GET STARTED

Begin by examining your facilities. How many bedrooms do you have? Are there any other rooms that can be converted? How about bathrooms? What are your kitchen facilities? How many people could you comfortably feed? The answers to these questions will help you determine how many guests you can accommodate at any one time.

One room in your home, perhaps the living room, should be made available as a community room, a place where the guests can congregate to watch television, play cards, or converse.

Depending upon the regulations of the community and state in which you live, it may be necessary to have an inspection of your premises. This will be concerned mainly with cleanliness and safety. It will be important to explain that you do not intend to run a nursing home, and thus will not require that type of license. There will be no medical treatment of your guests. For legal purposes you will be operating a boarding house.

Some communities require second story fire escapes on places of public accommodation. There are some relatively inexpensive ones on the market that, despite their low cost, meet all legal requirements.

SET "IN BETWEEN" RATES

Bear in mind that one of the attractions of your home is that it is not a nursing facility and therefore does not charge nursing home rates. You should be able to make a good profit by charging half what the nursing homes in your area do. But this will be considerably above boarding house rates because you'll be providing more service.

And what does this service consist of? Helping partially incapacitated guests in their dressing and grooming, for one thing. Assisting them in their personal hygiene, if necessary. Also paying special attention to their individual food needs and assisting those in wheelchairs or casts move about.

HOW TO OBTAIN GUESTS

In addition to the usual media advertising, you should seek referrals from physicians and hospitals. Invite them to pass the word on to people who might benefit from staying in such a home. It would also be worthwhile to contact senior citizens clubs. And you might borrow an attention-getting device from a nursing home in an eastern community that sponsors a senior citizens arts and crafts show each year. It's held at the nursing home so that the people who enter the competition must actually go there in order to compete. This brings the facility to the attention of a lot of people who might not otherwise be familiar with it.

TWO EXAMPLES OF SUCCESS

Mr. and Mrs. Ferdinand Alexander live in a suburban New York community and run a small rest home for senior citizens. They have one guest room on the ground floor and four on the second floor. Their guests are all ambulatory and able to go up and downstairs. The Alexanders' gross income from the project now averages over $1,000 monthly. Their out-of-pocket expenses total no more than $500. This leaves an excellent profit margin for the work involved.

In the northwest, a man has opened his farm to people who have been suffering from nervous exhaustion or mild depression. The simple, rural atmosphere and quiet surroundings allow them to forget problems for awhile. The cheerful manner in which the "rest farm" is operated helps give these people a new zest for living.

TEN MORE HOSPITALITY PROJECTS

Clubrooms. In the Midwest, a woman whose large home contains two kitchens rents out one of the kitchens and several of the adjoining rooms to club groups. Meetings, luncheons, and dinners keep the space well occupied, and the call for it has been so great that bookings must be made several months in advance.

Recording Studio. In New Jersey, a man whose hobby is sound recording equipped a small studio in his home and records local musical and theatrical groups as well as individual musicians and singers. The artists are provided with tapes of their performances. If they request, arrangements can be made to have the tapes transferred to disc.

Plant Hotel. A lady in Missouri earns a few extra dollars each week by tending plants in her home. They are deposited there by families departing on extended vacations.

Temporary Office Space. A house located on the main street of a bustling southwestern community is the focal point of nearly all of that community's charity drives and political campaigns. A number of ground floor rooms are made available to serve as headquarters for these efforts.

Study Center. Some working mothers prefer not to have their children return to an empty home after school, so they send them to after school study centers. Because a large number of students can be accommodated with minimal supervision, the fee is small and thus within reach of all families wishing the service.

Records Storage. Many firms that must keep voluminous files that are not often referred to welcome the opportunity to store them in locations where the rental is less than in the downtown business district. A number of homeowners with spare rooms have profited from filling this need.

Classroom Space. Instructors in such fields as music, dancing, and foreign languages frequently don't find it convenient to carry out their instruction in their homes. If you have several spare rooms and are centrally located, this is a potential source of income.

Rehearsal Hall. Musical organizations that play for catered affairs and at nightspots need a place where they can practice. A large room in your home can fit the bill and provide extra dollars for you.

Professional Office. Many homeowners living in the central areas of their communities have converted part of the ground floor levels of their homes for professional office use. Tenants include doctors, lawyers, accountants, and real estate brokers. The rental can be better than if the same space were leased as living quarters.

Equipment Storage. If you've got a sizable plot of ground, it can be put to profitable use storing small boats out of season as well as travel trailers and other hobby and recreational equipment owned by apartment dwellers.

Making Food
Your Business

Food probably offers a greater variety of money-making opportunities than any other category in this book. Why? Because food is a daily requirement for all of us, and we meet that requirement in many different ways.

We eat at home, using food bought at the corner grocery; we dine in restaurants; we grab a sandwich at the highway diner; we buy a hot dog from a street vendor; we put a dime in a slot machine for a candy bar . . . the list goes on and on.

It's safe to say that we buy food more often, and in more different ways, than any other item. And, human nature being what it is, we usually try to *vary* the type of food and the circumstances in which we eat it.

CAPITALIZE ON QUALITY
THE BIG FIRMS CAN'T AFFORD

Because of this craving for new food experiences, the field will always be open to those who can provide the unusual, exotic, or exceptional. The possibilities for people working at home are vast and the chances for achieving outstanding success are excellent when the products have a "home-made" quality that exceeds that of the mass production items flooding the market today.

Quality is, after all, the one factor that has continually spelled success for home-based food entrepreneurs. No large firm, not even the biggest food giant in the world, can hope to compete for excellence with the small company that turns out its products by hand.

In fact, some of the big food firms got their start as one-man (or woman) operations with a reputation for superiority. An example is the story of Pepperidge Farm founder Margaret Rudkin, with whom you'll become familiar later on in this chapter.

THOUSANDS OF SUCCESS STORIES
GUIDE YOUR WAY

But the story of Margaret Rudkin, although spectacular, is only one of many. Look around you in your own community. Count the nearby businesses based on food. Then try to imagine all of the behind-the-scenes firms that supply these stores, restaurants, and other purveyors of our daily bread. The figure would be staggering.

Where does the person working at home fit into all of this? Thousands of people in all parts of the land fit in very well, providing products and services that go (a) directly to the consumer or (b) to the retail establishments that serve the consumer.

The plans in this chapter were drawn from some of the most outstanding food enterprises being operated from private homes today.

12 RULES FOR A SUCCESSFUL FOOD PROJECT

While the variety of food projects with which you can make money is immense, there are certain techniques and rules that are common to nearly all. The 12 contained here are drawn from the most successful home-based food enterprises now in operation.

1. Establish a high standard of quality. It's the one feature on which no large firm can top you.

2. Be *consistent* in meeting the quality standards you have set. Have written records of the ingredients and procedures used in the preparation of your various products; thus customers will know from purchase to purchase that they are obtaining the same fine items.

3. Strive for the *unusual* whenever possible. Because people seek

variety in their food, the person who can provide it holds a distinct advantage.

4. Ascertain the market for your food product or service. Test it on a small scale to determine consumer acceptance.

5. Make your "package" (be it a cookie box or a restaurant building) as attractive as possible. This will make its contents that much more enticing.

6. Choose a piquant name. People buy food not merely for sustenance, but also because of its appetizing nature. Psychologists will confirm that the more attractive the name, the more tempting the item.

7. Establish your own "mass production" techniques. You need not sacrifice quality in order to increase your efficiency. Plan ahead and work out time and step-saving procedures.

8. Don't hesitate to hire help when needed. Limiting yourself to a one-person operation can cost you a sizable proportion of your potential profit.

9. Always perform as promised. Your customers must be able to count on delivery as scheduled.

10. Check health, sanitary, and legal requirements in your locality. Meeting these requirements will be easy—as long as you know what they are.

11. Be guided by your customers. If you're manufacturing food, or serving it, don't try to push your own favorites when customers obviously prefer something else. They are the best judges . . . push *their* favorites.

12. Charge well. The time, effort, and ingredients that go into providing top quality demand high rewards. Don't be afraid to charge for the full value of what you sell.

Plan 1: KITCHEN PRODUCTS

There's money in your kitchen, and thousands of women are taking advantage of this fact. Income from the sale of items produced in kitchens is helping to balance countless budgets, send numerous young people to college, and provide many families with luxuries they would not otherwise be able to afford.

Some kitchen enterprises have even grown into multi-million dollar industries. Although this may not be your goal, you can benefit from learning the techniques employed by such people as Mrs. Margaret Rudkin, who found herself in business almost before she knew it. It began when she worked up a special diet for a sickly son, and one item in that diet was a whole wheat bread baked from a recipe handed down by her grandmother.

She bought wheat from a local feed store and did the grinding in her kitchen coffee grinder. Abounding in natural vitamins and minerals, the bread was sure to help the youngster.

The good thing about this "medicine" was that Mark loved its taste. The family doctor recognized its benefits and suggested that Mrs. Rudkin provide him with some loaves for several other patients. She did, and also baked some loaves for a number of her friends.

After hearing a multitude of raves for her home-baked product, Mrs. Rudkin began to wonder whether or not she might be able to sell it. She baked eight loaves and took them to a storekeeper she knew in Fairfield, Connecticut, not far from her home. All eight were sold within a few hours, and the storekeeper put in a standing order. Then other storekeepers began requesting it, and Mrs. Rudkin hired a neighbor to help out.

The popularity of Pepperidge Farm Bread (named for the family farm) grew rapidly. The volume of sales reached 4,000 loaves the first year. By this time, of course, it was no longer produced in Mrs. Rudkin's kitchen, but strict control was maintained to assure continued high quality.

Sales now are well up in the millions of dollars per year. Its popularity has continued to climb, despite the fact that it costs more than regular bread.

A BABY-BASED BUSINESS

You have undoubtedly seen the magazine ads of Mrs. Dan Gerber, the woman who made a fortune out of an idea she had while mashing and straining vegetables for her infant daughter. This was in 1927, when doctors first recommended strained food for tots. There was none available on the market, and mothers spent much time preparing it.

Why not prepare it commercially? The idea was a good one, and the four varieties of strained fruits and vegetables sold extremely well. The success was almost unbelievable. A few ads inserted in women's magazines resulted in the sale of 2,400,000 units the first year.

HOW TO SELECT YOUR KITCHEN PRODUCT

There's hardly a housewife who doesn't have at least one food item about which her family and friends rave. What is yours? A special cookie recipe? That much-enjoyed cake you prepare for special occasions? Your bread? Preserves you put up, or jams you make? Chances are that if your family and friends enjoy it, other people will be more than willing to pay handsomely for it.

Determine how you can prepare this item in volume while maintaining the quality that has made it popular. Remember that your margin of profit will be determined by the amount of time that is required to produce each individual unit. In most food items, actual contents will be comparatively minor in relation to the cost of your own labor.

CHOOSE ONE OF THESE DISTRIBUTION METHODS

The nature of your product and the area in which you live will determine, to a large extent, how it is sold. Review each of these methods to find which fits best.

Roadside Stand. Many items sell well at stands located alongside well-traveled roads. Just a small supply atop a card table has launched many now-flourishing businesses. As the volume grows, usually a more permanent stand is erected.

In Illinois, Ellsworth Meineke began selling honey produced in his own hives at a roadside stand. Working full-time two months a year, he grossed over $4,650, but wasn't satisfied. This caused him to seek to make the honey more lucrative. He began making candy, with honey as the basic ingredient. This meant that instead of selling for 37¢ per pound, the honey-based product retailed at better than $1. Sales grew to more than 20,000 pounds per year.

Supplying Stores. Many kitchen-made products are retailed in local stores. You'll recall that Margaret Rudkin launched her Pepperidge Farm Bread in this manner.

It's easiest to launch your endeavor at the store in which you do your own shopping. Nine times out of ten the proprietor will be most happy to stock a trial supply. If it sells well, you're in business. As soon as one store is successfully handling your product, others will be willing to stock it as well.

In order to be assured of success in her first store trial, one woman in Pennsylvania notified all of her friends of the fact that the corner grocery was featuring her home-baked bread. This started the ball rolling, and it hasn't stopped yet. She now has ten stores on her list.

Mail Order. Non-perishable items often sell well through the mail. Many women's magazines contain mail shopping sections that are profitable sources of business. Sunday newspaper supplements also have shopping departments that are used by food dealers. A New England couple has been very successful marketing their maple syrup candies in this manner. Their advertising plays up the fact that the candy is made "in the heart of maple syrup country."

Supplying Restaurants. Restaurants that offer pies and cakes of home-baked quality find their patrons clamoring for more. Many women who supply restaurants with these items have discovered this to be a profitable fact of life.

Within a few miles of your home there are probably several restaurants that would welcome homemade cakes and pies to replace the tasteless cardboard variety so many have to settle for. You can start small by supplying just one establishment. Then, as the word spreads, so can your territory.

Plan 2: CATERING SERVICE

The customers provide the place and the occasion, you provide the food and perhaps the decorations; it's a combination that has been a winner for many at-home businessmen. And this *is*, basically, an at-home business, because that's where most of your work is done. The event at which the food is served is the culmination of considerable planning and effort for which you will have been well paid.

Catering services are being called on to handle all kinds of functions, from small, intimate family affairs to large corporate gatherings. You can specialize in one type of catering or spread throughout the entire field.

Let's take a look at the various categories:

Private Parties. Some families are prolific party-givers and are a constant source of profit for catering firms; others hire caterers for once-in-a-lifetime events to mark a very special occasion such as a golden wedding anniversary. The caterer provides anything from hors d'oeuvres to a full course meal, according to the customer's wishes. Most of the preparation takes place in the caterer's home and then the food is taken to the customer's home just prior to the event.

Weddings. Families that hold wedding receptions in their own homes or in church halls almost invariably depend upon caterers to take charge. Again, the affairs can range from the very simple to the very complex; from appetizers and unspiked punch (and a cake, of course) to a meal and flowing booze. Some caterers even arrange for the musical entertainment.

Business Receptions. When a firm opens a new branch, introduces a new product, hires a new president, or does anything else it wants to ballyhoo, it usually holds a party for its favored customers, representatives of the news media, and other individuals whose favor is being courted. Very often these affairs are held "on location," and the company depends on caterers to handle the arrangements. This is probably the most profitable of all types of catering, because budgets are less limited and the crowds are generally larger.

PICK YOUR SPECIALTY

The selection of the type of catering you'll be handling will be determined by a number of factors including the size and nature of the community in which you live, the availability of part-time help, your personal preference, and the amount and type of competition.

If you live in a metropolis, catering for commerce may be your choice. If, on the other hand, your community is rural or suburban in nature, you'll probably specialize in private affairs.

In any case, you'll want to line up part-time helpers on whom you can call. Work up a small list of assistants so that you'll never be short when their services are required.

HOW TO GET STARTED

Other than the usual media advertising, there are a number of advertising techniques that have proven especially effective for catering services. Some caterers have worked out arrangements with bake shops and delicatessens. All inquiries received at the stores are turned over to the service, with the understanding that the caterer will purchase the bulk of his food at the store from which the referral came.

In addition, these same stores willingly display posters advertising the catering firm, and insert brochures in bags of goods sold to their customers.

In states where it's legal, package stores will often permit similar advertising methods under the same arrangement.

A simple brochure can be distributed to the business firms in your operating territory that are potential customers of your service. These same brochures can also be mailed to the parents of brides-to-be when engagement announcements appear in the local newspapers.

HOW TO FIGURE YOUR CHARGES

Establishing fees is a skill that must be developed with experience. This means, of course, that you will have to tread with particular care in the beginning. Before giving a quote for an affair, figure all of your expenses (food, help, decorations, your time), include a safety margin of 10–15%, and then add a profit margin of about 30%.

You may be surprised, when the event is over, to find that "hidden" expenses have cropped up and inclusion of the safety margin was a wise move. A few parties later, you should be able to do away with that margin and also provide quotes with more rapidity.

The question of how much you can earn depends almost entirely on the degree of your ambition. One small affair per week can net you $20–$30. Your income can climb well up into the hundreds as the number and size of the events increase.

George Devereux, who launched a catering service in a fair-sized eastern community several years ago, is kept busy with an average of at least three assignments per week. He depends to a large extent on part-time employees to do the actual work while he does the quoting, planning, purchasing, and, of course, supervising.

Last year his profit reached five figures, and George tells me that he's now seriously considering giving up his regular job to run his business full time.

Plan 3: MEALS ON WHEELS

There's a profitable service you can provide for people who enjoy the comfort of eating at home but who occasionally want to avoid the bother of preparing a meal and washing the dishes. Offer them full meals delivered to their homes piping hot—at reasonable prices—and you can bet they'll become steady customers.

There is a similarity, and a dissimilarity, between this type of business and the various nationally-franchised firms that also feature home-delivered food.

The franchised operations specialize in one food, usually chicken, fish, or pizza. Whenever a customer phones in an order he has to settle for that one specialty.

Specializing in one food is the secret that has helped make these franchised firms successful. It's turned out on an assembly-line basis. There are few variations among orders. Because of the speed, mass-quantity purchasing, and the featuring of inexpensive main courses, the firms have been able to make good profits while holding their retail prices down.

Under the plan outlined here, you'll be able to adapt the best features of these nationally-known firms, but you also will be able to offer the variety they lack.

Your secret-of-success is that your menu will change from week to week. In any given week you will offer only one meal, and thus you will enjoy the advantages of mass production; but the following week you will have a different menu, providing variety for your customers. Like your franchised friend, one week you might feature chicken-in-the-basket; the following week, while he's featuring the same fare, you'll be offering ground beef, ham, meatloaf, or a casserole.

WHAT ARE THE REQUIREMENTS?

Provided you have the space, this enterprise can be launched at home. Possibly your present kitchen range will suffice, particularly if you intend to start very small and grow gradually. Or you might wish to pick up, second-hand, a restaurant-type stove for a hundred dollars or so and have it installed in a spare ground-floor room.

A minimum of two persons, including yourself, plus one motor vehicle will be needed. One person will handle the food preparation while the other uses the vehicle to make deliveries. The business can be started with an old (but reliable) station wagon or panel truck.

HOW TO BEGIN

1. Check your kitchen facilities. Have counter and storage space arranged so you can function with the most efficiency. Most of your orders will be handled in a three hour period, so you must be prepared to work rapidly. Step-saving will be the prime requisite.

2. Draw up three or four basic menus, featuring food that can be purchased inexpensively and that is easy to prepare. Along with your main course will go, usually, potatoes and another vegetable. You'll use paper plates and covered boxes, obtainable on a wholesale basis from a restaurant supply house. You'll also have a variety of beverages. These are the easiest to prepare, but surprisingly can account for much of your profit. Determine your cost for each menu, including containers and delivery within your operating radius (limited to a very few miles from your home).

3. Plan your delivery schedule. Most firms find it practical to send deliveries out once per hour, with each round trip designed to take no longer than 45 minutes. To illustrate, your deliveryman might plan to leave with orders every hour on the hour from five through nine P.M. After making his five o'clock deliveries, he'd be back to reload at 5:45. Any orders received prior to 5:30 would go out at six. Calls after 5:30 wouldn't go out until 7. Later, when your business increases and a second delivery vehicle is warranted, deliveries can be made more frequently.

4. Go through a trial run one night about a week before you accept your first orders. Have the deliveryman draw up a list of about

a dozen and a half orders. See how rapidly you can prepare them. Then you supply *him* with addresses. He'll have to drive to each (although not actually making the delivery, of course), and this will give you both a clear indication of any hitches that might need working out.

5. Order advertising in the local papers. Members of the ad staff will be glad to assist you in this. In your ads, be sure to list the complete menu for that week, the price, and the delivery area and schedule. This will save time when you receive phone orders. When the menu changes the following week, a new ad goes in the paper. You can also include the following week's menu, in mimeographed form, with each delivery. Eventually, you'll probably build up a customer list large enough to allow cutting down on the newspaper ads, with greater dependence on the flyers you include with the deliveries.

INVESTIGATE THESE
EXPANSION POSSIBILITIES

After your business is well established and running smoothly, you can begin to think of ways to make it even more profitable. They include:

1. Expanding the territory you serve
2. Accepting catering assignments during non-mealtime hours
3. Preparing "take-out" orders to be picked up by the customers
4. Moving the business to a commercial location in order to increase the take-out volume
5. Opening a branch in another territory

A TYPICAL ENTERPRISE

Several of these expansion moves were accomplished by Nick and Tony Potella in their meal delivery business. Starting from Nick's home with Nick doing the cooking and his brother the delivering, it wasn't long before Tony's son was enlisted as a second deliveryman and Nick's wife as an additional chef. This enabled them to begin serving a neighboring town as well as their own.

About a year later, the Potellas rented a small store, which allowed them to install pickup facilities. They even outfitted a small waiting room for customers who arrived without first phoning in their orders. Several vending machines in the waiting area add to the profits.

Their latest expansion step has been the opening of a branch in another part of the county in which they live.

Although the business began on a part-time basis, it has long since become a full-time enterprise, with the Potellas each netting more than $15,000 per year.

Plan 4: MOBILE REFRESHMENT UNIT

Every Saturday finds Al and Evelyn Desmond pleasantly occupied in an enterprise that adds about $85 to the family pocketbook. The income results from about seven hours of work per Saturday, preceded by about two hours on Friday night.

Mr. and Mrs. Desmond are earning their spare-time money by selling refreshments at public events. They have no special equipment other than a large folding table, a small ice chest, a coffee urn, and a cash box. Each Saturday morning the ice chest is filled with soda pop, the table loaded with sandwiches, pie, and cake, and the coffee urn set to perk at full steam. As the ice chest, table, and urn become depleted, the cash box becomes correspondingly full.

The Desmonds earn their profits by using the third in the following list of basic methods of profiting from mobile refreshment units:

1. Selling to travelers from a roadside location
2. Driving a daily route
3. Catering to public events

Let's examine each method individually.

FIND A BUSY ROADSIDE SPOT

Dominic C. purchased a small second-hand truck several years ago, painted it white, installed a grill and a cooler, and chose a picnic area on a main highway near his community. The picnic area, maintained by the state, has a magnificent view and is popular with the traveling public.

Dominic inquired with the state highway department and found that no special permit was required to use the state property. (There might, however, be such a requirement in your state.) There *were* certain health department requirements, but these apply to all mobile refreshment units and are easily complied with.

Dominic has taken his truck to that roadside rest area every day except Monday for the past three years (save for an annual three-week vacation) and even on the slowest, poor weather weekdays he clears at least $20. On Saturdays, Sundays, and holidays this figure is multiplied several times.

Although Dominic operates his business full time, many people handle similar enterprises solely on weekends and holidays. The secret lies in finding the right location. Not everyone will be as fortunate as Dominic in picking the proper spot the first time out. A bit of traveling back and forth and some comparison work at several locations may be necessary—and it will be well worthwhile.

TRAVEL A ROUTE

A recently-retired laundry routeman in the Midwest decided to fill his new-found free time by going into business for himself. He located a company in his city that leased foodmobiles for $17 per day, and he was soon earning a good income visiting the various construction sites in the city, providing the workers with hot coffee, soft drinks, sandwiches, and ice cream. Before long, they came to expect him at the same time each day, and he found that he could fairly well predict each day's sales in advance. This was helpful, for instead of making the sandwiches himself, he purchased them each morning on a wholesale basis from the company that leased the truck to him.

It is not unusual for a route operator to clear $200 per week from his business—but the hours can be long. Usually he must begin his work early in the morning and continue through mid-afternoon.

Many people who start out by leasing a fully-equipped truck eventually buy their own unit. A new one can cost upward of $10,000, but there are many good buys to be had second-hand.

FOLLOW THE SPECIAL EVENT TRAIL

Like Al and Evelyn Desmond, you may wish to work just one day per week. They made an arrangement a number of years ago with a local auctioneering firm to handle the lunch concession at the Saturday auctions. Some of the sales are held at residences, others at the auction barn. But wherever the auction is, there is bound to be a hungry crowd of at least 150 persons.

If the Desmonds didn't have their lucrative auction arrangement, they would not find it difficult to choose other public occasions where a lunch concession would be profitable. These include high school and college sporting events, parades, rallies, conventions—any activity where people gather. Events out-of-doors are usually best, because people tend to be hungrier and setting up your equipment is easier.

Each Friday afternoon, Evelyn purchases items needed for the next day's activity. That evening, she bakes several pies and cakes, and makes and wraps a pile of sandwiches.

On Saturday, when the sandwich pile gets near the bottom, they begin making more. In the rare instance when pies or cakes are left over at the end of the day, they sell them at reduced prices to people who wish to take them home.

Arrangements must usually be made in advance for permission to cater public events. Most often, permission is readily granted; in some cases it may be necessary to pay a small fee or commission to the sponsoring organization. This can actually be to your advantage, for it is a guarantee of exclusiveness—an assurance that there will be no competition.

Plan 5: MINI-RESTAURANT

When you think of the many restaurants that are located in former homes, it seems only logical that present homes could serve the same purpose. With so many eating places trying to *simulate* a home setting, the real thing can prove even more popular.

And such is the case in dozens of examples that I have studied. Homeowners with spare time and space are converting those two quantities into a surprisingly good source of added income by operating mini-restaurants in their homes.

How does a mini-restaurant differ from a regular restaurant? Only in scale. It's smaller, geared for more intimate dining. Otherwise it can match the best. Prices can range from very reasonable to the exorbitant, and the menu can be simple or extremely varied—depending on your own ideas and goals

You can begin with a staff of just two—one to be in charge of the kitchen, the other to wait on table. To accomplish this, you can enlist the aid of your spouse or a child in the upper teens.

The restaurant part of your home can be located in one large room, several smaller rooms—or in a large room created from what formerly were two or more smaller rooms.

HOW TO ATTRACT DINERS

The three factors that determine the popularity of any restaurant are (1) its food, (2) its atmosphere, and (3) its location. Let's consider them one by one and see how they apply to your mini-restaurant.

The Food. The small restaurants that do best are generally those that specialize in a particular type of food, such as that of a foreign nation, or in certain native specialities, i.e., steaks, seafood, etc. After choosing your specialty, try to choose a restaurant name that points up that specialty.

The Atmosphere. Many diners choose their restaurants on the basis of atmosphere more than anything else, so give careful thought to how you decorate your dining area, and to the layout of its tables and chairs. Naturally, the motif should match your food specialty as closely as possible. If you feature seafood, give your rooms a nautical air. If it's foreign fare that you offer, give your establishment touches that hint of that land.

The Location. Since you'll be operating from your home, there's nothing you can do to improve your location. If you're on a main highway, fine; if not, you'll have to make your restaurant so enticing that diners will beat a path to your door. This is not as difficult as it sounds. People in search of good food and warm surroundings are accustomed to going to out-of-the-way places. Sometimes it even contributes to the atmosphere.

HOW TO GET STARTED

Here's a five-point program for getting your own mini-restaurant established:

1. Decide on the layout of your restaurant, taking best advantage of your available space. Where rooms have large inter-connecting

archways, very little usually has to be done in the way of structural changes. In other cases, however, it may be necessary to tear out the connecting wall to make one large dining area. Have restroom facilities close at hand. Organize your kitchen for efficient food production.

2. Pick a specialty, and base your decor on that. This is the most important aspect of planning your business, so do it carefully. Decide on your hours of operation. Most mini-restaurants are open only for dinner, generally from 5 to 9 weekdays and perhaps in the early afternoon on Sundays.

3. Install your equipment, including the dining tables and chairs, serving buffets, etc. Most of these items should probably be purchased second-hand. Since the tables will be kept covered most of the time, their condition is not overly important, and they need not match.

4. Obtain whatever local food-serving permits are required. Inquire at the health department to determine just what the requirements are. Your kitchen will be subject to inspection, so be sure it's spotless.

5. Start advertising. The number one item, of course, is a sign out front. Then come some ads in the local paper to announce that you are open. You might supplement these with ads in regional diners' guides and tourist directories. Many small restaurants find that they need advertise only at the outset. Because of their limited capacity, their tables are thereafter kept full with repeat customers and those who have heard about the restaurant from friends.

16 MORE FOOD PROJECTS

There's practically no end to the ways in which you can earn money in food projects. But here are some examples from my files:

Hors d'oeuvres. An ingenious woman living in a suburban area noted the large number of receptions and cocktail parties being given for promotional purposes by local business concerns. Why not go into the hors d'oeuvres business? She found there was a definite market for her products, which are ordered in advance and then picked up at her home.

Salads. A lady in Wisconsin became locally famous for the quality of her salads. But how does one sell salads? After some thinking, she decided to ask the local delicatessen owner if he'd put some in his display case. He agreed somewhat hesitantly—then quickly called for more when he saw how well it sold.

Ice Cream. Did you ever churn homemade ice cream as a child? Remember its unique flavor—something never found in the aerated commercial products on the market today? A man in Rhode Island remembered, and he got a local store to take some of his homemade ice cream on a trial basis. It sells for considerably more than the factory-made variety, but customers clamor for it.

Regional Specialties. Many home businesses are based on regional foods. Maple syrup and its by-products provide one example, apple cider another. Depending on the nature of the product, they can be sold from roadside stands or through the mail.

Meals to Order. This is something like Plan 3, except that the preparation is more individualized and the price accordingly higher. This plan is popular in resort areas where people renting cottages don't have the facilities or inclination to cook large meals. Offer two or three basic meals and let your customers take their choice. Delivery is not a must; a number of women operating this type of business require that the meals be picked up at their kitchen doors.

Fresh Citrus Juice. There are still restaurants that prefer to bypass the frozen variety and serve just-squeezed fruit juice. With the proper juice-making equipment in your home, you can accommodate them profitably, delivering the juice in large glass jugs.

Fruitcake. Fruitcakes and nutcakes are excellent mail order sellers, especially in the gift line. Businessmen like to send them to their clients. Your advertising is aimed at these businessmen, and with each new customer you usually sell several cakes. Brochures sent to each *recipient* with his gift are the source of future orders.

Box Lunches. Factory and office workers can provide you with steady income if you prepare tasty lunches for them to take to work. Vary the menu from day to day, include soup as a frequent supplement to sandwiches and fruit, and your customers will come back for more.

Wedding Cakes. They're big and they're profitable. A woman in Kentucky is said to supply 75% of all the wedding cakes in her community. Sales are made directly to the family, or to the restaurant in which the reception is held.

Mini-Mini-Restaurant. This is Plan 5 on an even smaller scale. A number of home-located restaurants function on a one-day-per-week basis. Examples: Sunday brunch; Saturday night home-cooked meals for collegiates; Friday night fish-fries.

Commission Sales. There are many women who would like to earn money from their homemade foodstuffs, but who don't want to get involved in selling it. A shop in your home can feature the various items prepared by women in your neighborhood. A 25% commission will amply repay you for your effort.

Casseroles. In Minnesota, "Cora's Casseroles" is the name of a profitable enterprise operated by a woman who provides this type of food on order. The service is popular with families that have unexpected guests, housewives who want to stay out of the kitchen for a night, people who are just moving in or out of their homes, etc.

Candy Fund-Raisers. A popular method of raising funds for a worthwhile cause is to sell candy door-to-door. A number of women who have especially good candy recipes have worked out arrangements with local organizations. They supply the candy in volume at sufficient discount to provide profit for the organization when its members peddle it. The homemaker can devote most of her time to preparing the candy, with only minimal administrative details to attend to.

Tea Time. Opening her living room for gatherings of women's groups, and serving tea and other light refreshments, is the basis of a profitable enterprise conducted by a California resident.

Garden Produce. Housewives still prefer home-grown fruits and vegetables when they're available. Sell from a roadside stand or through local stores. It's a seasonal source of extra income that continues to flourish in various parts of the country.

Cooking School. Many high schools offer home economics courses, but you'd be surprised at the number of brides-to-be who elected not to take them and are suddenly desirous of improving their cooking skills. Small classes of three or four girls are best. You can operate from your own kitchen, or arrange to go to the home of one of your students.

10

How to Manage
an External Enterprise
from Your Home

Even though your goal is to make money at home, there is no rule saying every aspect of your business must be confined to your own four walls. Many people use their homes as "head offices" for outside enterprises of the type that do not require constant personal supervision. These include ventures that are essentially self-service in nature, and those in which the locations can vary from day to day.

EARN HANDSOME REWARDS
FOR YOUR MANAGERIAL SKILLS

In most external enterprises, you are not involved in the act of making or repairing things, so income is not limited by your physical capacity to produce. The extent of the profit depends more on your managerial decisions than on how fast your fingers can fly.

Don't let this frighten you. Most good business decisions involve no more than common sense and perhaps a little foresight. And even foresight itself generally requires no more than analyzing a given set of circumstances.

An example is provided in the story of Harry G., who owned a laundromat in a small college town. His lease was about to expire and Harry was faced with having to make a decision on whether to renew for another three years or to move a block away to an available location that was large enough to accommodate twice as many machines.

Moving a laundromat is no easy or inexpensive task, so the decision had to be well thought out. Harry knew that the college was expanding its graduate school, and he reasoned that there would be an influx of young couples moving into apartments in the town. Already some of the large old homes were being converted into apartments.

Although his 14-machine laundromat was rarely in full use at that time, Harry reasoned that with the arrival of a lot more young marrieds, the demand for coin-operated washing machines would rise sharply. He moved to the larger quarters, and his foresight has paid off very well.

MAKE YOUR KITCHEN TABLE
AN ADMINISTRATION CENTER

Because most external enterprises don't require your physical presence on a day-to-day basis, a large proportion of your involvement is in handling administrative details, and this is usually accomplished at home. Thus, your kitchen table (or desk in the den) literally does become an administration center.

You work the hours that are most convenient for you, and if you don't feel like working at all one day you can generally put the tasks off to another day.

And because in most cases customers won't be coming to your home, there's no need to put on a "front" and fix up any fancy reception area. You can work in your shirtsleeves—or pajamas, if you wish.

MULTIPLY YOUR PROFITS
WITH MULTIPLE PROJECTS

Many entrepreneurs operate several external enterprises simultaneously. This is possible because so many businesses in this category require comparatively little "in person" attention.

After you've established one business and have it functioning on a profitable basis, you can expand your scope by launching new projects. These can be of the same type (Harry G., for instance, now owns *several* laundromats) or they can be in an entirely different field.

So, when you've found a plan in this chapter that appeals to you, don't shut your mind off from the others. You may want to review them later when your ambition starts to itch and you begin thinking about additional profit projects.

Plan 1: RENTAL REAL ESTATE

William Nickerson retired from the telephone company at the age of 42 to live off the income of the wealth he had accumulated in his spare time. He amassed that wealth starting with an investment of just $1,000. He has told the complete story in two books, *How I Turned $1,000 into Three Million in Real Estate—in My Spare Time,* and *How to Make a Fortune Today, Starting from Scratch,* both published by Simon and Schuster.

But William Nickerson isn't the only man who's done it—not by a long shot. Thousands upon thousands of Americans, people who knew little or nothing about real estate at the start, today are doing very well through their ownership of residential income property. And the wonderful thing is that it is possible to start, as Nickerson says, "from scratch."

Robert W. Kent has made himself a millionaire this way, and he's taught others to do the same thing. He tells the story of a man who had immigrated to the land of opportunity only to establish himself in a very meager-paying position in a chain store. He asked Kent if it would be possible for him to repeat Kent's great success in rental properties. Kent agreed to show him how, and reports that within ten years his friend was close to his first million and now has far surpassed it.

Kent's formula for success is contained in *How to Get Rich in Real Estate,* published by Prentice-Hall, Inc.

While differing in their systems, Nickerson and Kent have followed the same basic route to fortune: They have pyramided their holdings.

Nickerson suggests that you begin by purchasing a two-family home with a minimum down payment, improve its value through renovations, and then sell it at a profit. This profit is then used as the down payment for a larger building. This building, in turn, is improved and sold at a profit, and once again the profit is plowed back into your venture for the purchase of a still larger structure. You gradually increase your holdings in this manner.

The secret of all this is leverage. Nickerson says he started with a thousand dollars, but recommends today that $2,500 would be a more realistic figure.

Actually, it's possible to start with nothing. Many have done it. Usually, a first mortgage can be obtained from a lending institution for up to 75% of the purchase cost of the building. Then the seller often is willing to take back a second mortgage for a substantial part of the remainder, if not all of it.

Kent pyramids in another way. He's an advocate of purchasing three-family homes and holding on to them. He advises buying them in good livable condition, or making them that way, but from then on providing only minimum maintenance. The theory behind this is that you are not trying to improve their value, but to have them provide a good rental income over a period of many years.

At first, all of your profits would be plowed back, not in improvements as Nickerson suggests, but in purchases of additional three-family units.

FOLLOW THE VALUE FORMULA

But no matter which method you follow, there is one requirement that must always be met: The property must be of the type that will at least maintain, if not improve, its value. A beautiful house in a slum area would be a poor investment. A rundown house in a good neighborhood would be far better.

The prime factor in determining value, therefore, is location. But even after you have found a building that is well located, you still must be able to establish its value in dollars so you can determine how much you should pay. One generally accepted standard is that a building is worth about six and two-thirds times its gross annual rental. Another is that it's worth about ten times its net annual rental (the figure arrived at after taxes, insurance, and other expenses are deducted).

RELY ON A BROKER

At this point you may be saying, "This all sounds well and good, but I've had no experience in real estate. How do I go about finding property, and how do I arrange a mortgage?"

The answer is to get in touch with a realtor—a member of your city or county board of realtors. After showing you the properties he has listed, he can usually help you arrange all of the financing. It's part of his service, and it costs you nothing since his commission is paid by the seller.

You can learn much about real estate by studying the classified advertising columns of a fairly large newspaper. These often contain many offerings of income property, usually listed under "Investment Property" or "Apartment Houses."

Even if you're not ready to make a purchase, answer a few of the ads and inspect the properties. The seller doesn't know whether or not you are really in the market, and he'll be glad to give you a tour of the premises and present all of the working figures. This will provide you with a valuable education in real estate and before long you will have developed a keen sense of value.

Plan 2: VENDING MACHINES

For three reasons, operating a vending machine route is one of the most popular of all external enterprises.

The reasons are these:

1. The machines are independent money-makers, attracting coins day after day, requiring only a minimum of attention from the route operator.

2. The overhead is low in contrast to most businesses. The chief overhead items are machine depreciation, commissions to location owners, repairs, and mileage.

3. Once a good location is established, it can be profitable indefinitely. Indeed, the location is the most important factor in determining profitability.

CHOOSE FROM A WIDE ARRAY OF MACHINES

Every year, new items are being added to the list of products sold through vending machines. But a dozen types of vending machines seem to remain constantly at the top of the hit parade. They are the ones that sell cigarettes, soda pop, candy, music (juke boxes), coffee, milk, prepared foods (sandwiches, etc.), hot canned foods, ice cream, cigars, novelties, games (amusement devices).

The cost of these machines can range from $25 or so up into the thousands. At the low end are dispensers of candy and novelties; at the high end are juke boxes, soda machines, and those that dispense hot foods.

Thus, you've got to decide whether you want to begin on a limited scale with inexpensive machines while you learn the ropes of operating a vending machine route, or if you are willing to invest (and risk) a more sizable sum of money.

WHAT TO LOOK OUT FOR

Because of the obvious attractions of this type of endeavor, many people have lost money by "jumping in" without really investigating. They have been lured by companies promising fantastic profits but delivering only vastly over-priced machines.

That's why it's imperative to check out *several* companies in the field you are considering. Only in this way can you determine the real value of the equipment you purchase.

Another manner in which neophyte route operators have been defrauded has been in the promises from the machine sellers that top-notch locations would be established for the operator. Very often these locations have turned out to be third-rate, if any have been arranged at all.

Any reputable firm will be glad to provide you with the names of some of its other route operators in your region. This will enable you to check with these people to see if they have been satisfied in their dealings with the company.

Another thing to check before purchasing machines is the availability of repair parts.

MEET THESE SUCCESS REQUIREMENTS

As mentioned before, your first consideration after deciding on the type of machine is placement. There are three basic categories: Retail stores; traffic centers such as depots, hotels, and theaters; and large places of employment.

The owners of these establishments are paid commissions based on the gross receipts of the vending machines. These commissions range from 2% to more than 25%, depending on the type of item being sold. The commission paid for about half of all vending machines now in use is reported to be 10%.

It is often advisable to obtain a signed contract from a location owner before placing machines on his premises. Contract forms can usually be obtained from machine manufacturers. You may want to have your attorney examine and possibly adapt these standard forms.

You must be able to maintain the machines yourself—at least at the outset. Having to hire a mechanic every time there is a malfunction can drain your profits more rapidly than anything else. Many manufacturers operate training schools, and you should certainly take advantage of them.

Most of your breakdowns will be simple to correct, especially with the less complex, non-electrical machines. But be thoroughly familiar with your equipment so that you can handle 99% of all the trouble that does occur.

As with any business, quality and service are musts. The products you offer in your machines must be of good quality, or complaints from customers will convince the owner to have the machines removed. Service is equally important; the owner will expect the machines to be re-stocked regularly and repaired promptly.

DIVERSIFICATION IS THE KEY

Many vending machine operators are earning particularly good profits by diversifying. This allows them to install several different types of vending machines in each location. Among the advantages are the mileage savings in servicing the route operator's total inventory of machines, and the ability to capitalize on locations that have proven especially good by adding additional machines as warranted.

Plan 3: AUCTIONEERING

The cry of "Going, going, gone" can mean money in your pocket—a surprisingly lot of it. Auction businesses are earning good profits in countless communities across the continent. Large towns, small towns, cities—all are good locations for a properly-run auction enterprise.

TWO NEIGHBORS STRIKE IT RICH

A typical example is the experience of Richard Holmes and James Tiscera, two neighbors who were appointed to the fund-raising committee of their local Parent-Teacher Association. Little did they realize how greatly that volunteer assignment would change their lives.

One of them would be able to send three children through college and purchase a lovely new home in a smart section of town because of what developed from his service on that committee. The other put a large addition on his house one year and had the entire structure refurbished the next—improvements he had long dreamed about but had not really held out any hope for.

The fund-raising committee to which Dick and Jim were appointed decided to conduct an auction, and Dick and Jim were selected to be the auctioneers. The plan was to canvass homes in the community and seek donations of unwanted furniture and household items. These were taken to the school auditorium shortly before the Saturday of the sale.

Prior to that day, neither Dick nor Jim had ever been to an auction, let alone conducted one. Yet they found it easy, holding up or pointing to the merchandise and inviting bids from the audience. Dick worked the auction block during the morning hours, and Jim in the afternoon. At the end of the day, the PTA scholarship fund was richer by more than $1100. Dick and Jim met at their common back yard fence the next day and exchanged amazement at how well the event had gone.

It was over that fence that a highly successful partnership was formed. Dick and Jim reasoned that if the PTA could do so well in the auction business, they could, too.

There was, of course, one obstacle. They weren't the PTA, and thus would not be able to obtain salable items for nothing.

CONSIGNMENT SELLING IS THE ANSWER

"Then Jim hit upon an idea," Dick explains. "He figured that many people with items to dispose of would be willing to have us sell them on a commission basis. This would work to our advantage because we would not have to make an investment, and to the seller's advantage because he'd know that we'd do our darnedest to get the best possible price in order to draw a good commission."

They found a local church that was willing to rent out its social hall on a Saturday for $15, provided the Ladies Aid could have the food concession. With the hall reserved about a month in advance, Dick and Jim went about getting items to sell. They inserted a small classified ad in the paper:

> Wanted: Used Furniture,
> antiques, household items,
> and tools to sell at auction.
> Let us dispose of your un-
> wanted items for you. Tel.
> 000-0000.

Both men were pleased (and even a bit surprised) at the number of persons who responded. But they soon learned that many of the people had no way to get items to the church hall. A plan was worked out. Those who could transport their own items would take them to the church hall the Friday night before the sale. Dick and Jim would be on hand to receive them. People who had no transportation were told it could be arranged at a fee that would be deducted from the selling price.

They found that by two weeks prior to the sale more than enough goods had been promised. A list was made of the better pieces, and this was included in a small $15 display advertisement announcing the sale. The ad was inserted in each of the newspapers printed within a radius of about 20 miles.

They conducted the sale much as they had for the PTA—one working in the morning, the other in the afternoon. The man who was not on the block served as a "runner," delivering sold items to the customers in the audience and collecting the money. Wisely, they had arranged to have a hired helper on hand so that while one man made a delivery the other could hold up the next item to be sold.

There was one other employee: Jim's wife, who sat at a small table near the auction block and recorded the price at which each item was sold.

The auction went very well in view of the fact that it was their first commercial attempt. Here are the figures:

Expenses		*Income*	
Advertising	$60	Gross sales	$995
Hall rental	15	Less 75% to	
Help	24	sellers	746
Miscellaneous	20		$249
	$119		

Subtract the expenses from the commission received, and you arrive at $130, or $65 apiece, which is not bad for the first time. Naturally, the profits increased with each succeeding sale as the partners became more efficient and their business became better known.

They soon developed a mailing list of those who attended their sales. This enabled them to cut down on their newspaper advertising.

MORE MONEY FOR LESS WORK

Before long they conducted their first house sale—an auction of all the goods in a home, conducted on the lawn of the premises. They found that such sales required less work since there was less juggling of furniture, and brought more money because customers paid higher prices when they saw items coming directly out of a home. And of course there was no rent to pay.

YOU CAN DO THE SAME

The success achieved by Dick and Jim is not unusual. The secret, as with most enterprises in this book, is to start small and feel your way along, gaining experience as you go. As Dick and Jim learned, initial experience is not necessary—but it would be helpful to attend auctions, if you can, to see how others operate.

No business address other than your home is needed, since all preliminary arrangements can be handled from there, and the actual sales will be conducted from a rented hall or at the house from which the goods are being sold.

When your business grows sufficiently, you can, if you wish, obtain your own premises and go full time.

One such auctioneer bought an abandoned church. He holds auctions there on Saturdays and sells "over-the-counter" during the week.

Plan 4: FRANCHISING

There are scores of low investment, part-time franchised businesses that you can operate from your home, and thousands of people are deriving excellent incomes this way. Most of the enterprises do require some travel about the community—but the franchises referred to here rarely entail rental of business or commercial space.

Why a franchise? For one thing, when you deal with a reputable franchisor you are given thorough training and you follow a proven program that has already made money for others just like you. For another, you benefit from the franchisor's nationally-known name and reputation. And a third reason is the leverage that is often available to you. Because the franchisor is frequently willing to provide quite a bit of financing, you get into a franchised business for far less initial investment than would be required if you were to do it on your own.

Still another attraction is the fact that the failure rate for franchised businesses is phenomenally low. This is something to consider if the idea of taking risks in a business of your own gives you even a hint of the shakes.

CHOOSE FROM A WIDE ASSORTMENT

You may be pleasantly surprised to learn of the many types of business available to you through franchising—even when you limit yourself to low investment plans in which your home can serve as headquarters. Here's just a partial list:

Accounting and Tax Service	Health Products and Services
Advertising Services	Home Maintenance and Equipment
Automotive Products	
Building Services and Products	Industrial Products
Business Services	Lawn Care
Cleaning and Maintenance Services	Mail Order Plans
	Rental Services
Collection Services	Rug and Upholstery Cleaning
Correspondence Schools	Self Service Laundries
Employment Agencies	Sports and Recreation
Fire and Burglary Protection	Vending Machines

"All right," you say, "sounds O.K. so far—but why would a big national company want to set *me* up in business?" One of the chief values of the franchise system is that it allows a company to have many more branches than would probably be possible otherwise. Rather than having to manage and operate hundreds of thousands of branches across the country, keeping extremely close tabs on all of them, it can go into "partnership" with local franchisees. Since the franchisee wants to make money, he'll try harder than a paid manager who has no profit motive.

This works out well both ways. You gain from the company's knowledge, name, and experience; the company gains by having you conduct its operation in your community.

"INVESTIGATE BEFORE YOU INVEST"

The quote comes from "the bible" on franchising, *The Franchise Boom* by Harry Kursh, published by Prentice-Hall, Inc. The book is full of advice on how you can profit in the boom, as well as the pitfalls to avoid. It also lists numerous franchise firms in all categories.

Mr. Kursh's advice about investigating is correct. Don't let the many success stories achieved by others in franchising draw you into a plan that doesn't fit you. Learn as much as you can about a franchise before you sign up for it. Visit several different operators and seek candid information on their experiences.

In addition to *The Franchise Boom,* you should subscribe to the newsletter, *National Franchise Reports,* published at 333 North Michigan Avenue, Chicago, Illinois 60601. Here you'll find monthly reports on the latest offerings, plus an annual booklet listing hundreds of opportunities.

An annual publication that also lists numerous franchises, along with brief descriptions, is the *Directory of Franchising Organizations* published by Pilot Industries, 347 Fifth Avenue, New York, New York 10016.

Plan 5: APARTMENT HOUSE MANAGEMENT

As explained in Plan 1 in this chapter, thousands of Americans are investing in apartment houses. There is a business you can conduct by performing a valuable service for apartment house owners. You can earn a good part-time or full-time income serving as manager of one or even many apartment buildings.

Apartment managers are needed because many of the owners are not in a position to manage their own units. They may live in a distant city or they may be too busy to handle the details, but in any event they are willing to pay five per cent of the total rent roll, and sometimes more, for someone else to do it for them.

Just what does an apartment house manager do? It varies with the specific agreement, but in most cases the duties are these:

Collect monthly rents
Obtain new tenants to fill vacancies
Oversee maintenance of premises
Keep financial records
Study means of increasing efficiency
Make recommendations for improvement

Generally, there are two types of owner-management relationship. In one, the manager takes almost complete responsibility for the apartment house. He acts as if he were the owner, and in addition to the above duties, he sees that bills and taxes are paid, and insurance is kept up-to-date. Very often the income is deposited in his own account, from which he pays all expenses, deducts his commission, and transmits a check for the balance to the owner, along with a complete accounting.

In the second type of owner-manager relationship, all bill-paying is handled by the owner, and the owner is also responsible for such details as meeting the mortgage payments and paying for insurance and taxes, although the manager might give occasional reminders or turn over specific bills to him.

The latter plan is better for someone just starting out in real estate management. It will provide you with the basic experience needed before you become totally involved.

ENJOY SEVERAL SOURCES OF INCOME

The wonderful thing about real estate management is that you can take on many jobs. Francis L., a resident of New York, manages five apartment buildings having a combined monthly rent roll of $12,500.

This means he receives $625 per month in commission, which is not bad for a 20-hour-per-week enterprise.

HOW TO OBTAIN ASSIGNMENTS

Many owners of apartment houses turn to real estate agents to take care of their buildings, but you will be able to offer more individualized service because this will be your main interest, not selling buildings or property.

All investors in real estate make regular checks of the *wanted* and *for sale* columns in the real estate classified sections of their newspapers. If they're looking for a manager, they'll respond to an ad in the same section reading like this:

> Real Estate Manager available to assume management of your apartment house. Competent, friendly service, commission basis. Phone 000-0000.

You can also write to various realtors in your area, telling them of your service and asking that they pass your name along to purchasers of apartment buildings. You might get in touch with persons who have inserted *apartments for rent* ads in the paper. Some will be tired of handling the rental and management duties by themselves.

HOW TO CARRY OUT YOUR DUTIES

Your job will be much easier if you make a practice of giving the owner a monthly report (many require this anyway). This will include information on which apartments are rented, what the rent roll amounts to (for each unit and totally), out-of-pocket expenses you have incurred, special services for which you have contracted, situations that warrant action, and general recommendations.

How and by whom the maintenance and repair tasks are performed will be in accordance with the understanding you have with your client. The cost will be over and above your commission. If you do the work yourself, you will expect just compensation; if you retain someone else to do it, his bill will be paid out of the building's maintenance fund. In either case, it will be your responsibility to see that the work gets done.

"Seeing that the work gets done" will require frequent trips to the premises—on a weekly basis, at the least. You will check for burned-out hall lights, litter and/or dirt, broken windows, peeling paint, unsafe conditions, etc. Your goal is to trouble the owner with these matters as little as possible.

CHECK THE ORDINANCES

Before going into business, check state and local requirements. While regulations vary, absentee managers are usually permitted in all but the largest buildings. You may choose, however, to accept a large building as one of your assignments—and the apartment that goes with it. The rental value will, of course, be considered part of your compensation.

PUT YOUR KNOWLEDGE
TO OTHER PROFITABLE USES

A by-product of the knowledge you'll gain is the ability to recognize profitable apartment house operations. Investment property can often be bought with very little down payment, sometimes with practically none at all, and unusually profitable opportunities may present themselves to you.

NINE MORE EXTERNAL ENTERPRISES

Party Plans. Many nationally-known manufactures and/or distributors of home products, jewelry, cosmetics, etc., have party plans in which their agents in the community conduct parties at private homes. Those who attend are treated to refreshments and demonstrations of the product. Then they are invited to purchase. As the agent, you arrange to conduct such parties in homes in various sections of the community. Firms featuring party plans advertise regularly in the salesmen's magazines, so check one of these.

Exterminating. Whether or not we like to admit it, just about all of us have, at one time or another, need for an exterminator to rid our homes of unwanted pests. How do you obtain the necessary knowledge and skill to fill this need? Write the U.S. Agriculture Department's Bureau of Entomology and Plant Quarantine for a list of publications on the subject. Also, your local bookstore has a catalog in which you can check for related tomes.

Business Brokerage. Bringing together buyers and sellers of business firms can be extremely profitable. The commission goes up to 10%. In many areas, no brokerage license is required—but check local ordinances. By following up ads and doing a lot of legwork, you can build a file of sellers' offerings and buyers' wants that can put many thousands of extra dollars in your pocket each year.

Weight Reducing Club. Provided you have no extra cleavage yourself, you can rent a hall and form a club of fat ladies who'd like to become *formerly* fat ladies. You supervise weekly programs of inspiration and guidance, and collect a fee from each person who attends. A Stop Smoking Club can be launched in the same manner.

Fund Raising. You can keep up to 25% of the "take" if you can dream up effective fund-raising activities for local clubs and organizations. How do you do it? By arranging mini-carnivals, entertainment galas, game nights, etc.

Car Washes. You've seen those 25-cent car wash machines at service stations. Many of the machines are not owned by the service station operators, but by entrepreneurs who have arranged to install them there, paying the station owners a commission of the gross. You can purchase these machines outright from the manufacturers, or you can handle it on a franchise basis (see Plan 4).

Ice Stations. Machines that sell ice are usually very profitable. After all, a cheaper basic ingredient is hard to find. Place a number of them in and around your community, service them regularly, and you've got a good source of extra income.

Rack Merchandising. Numerous wholesalers and distributors prefer to sell their products from special displays, or racks, placed in retail stores. These firms seek local residents to manage the racks, refilling them as necessary and collecting the money for the items sold. If this type of business appeals to you, check any of the salesmen's magazines for the latest offerings.

Adult Education Course. Adults seeking to upgrade their knowledge and ability in such fields as dancing, public speaking, and foreign languages are often willing to pay good tuitions when an effective course is offered. By renting a small hall and hiring a knowledgeable instructor (or doing it yourself if you can) you'll be on the way toward developing a welcome source of profit. Try not to duplicate any course that is offered as an adult ed item in your local school system; it will be impossible for you to offer a competitive tuition schedule.

11

Operating a
Specialized Help
Agency

First of all, a definition: A specialized help agency is a service which can be called upon to provide workers, generally on a temporary or sporadic basis, in one particular field of endeavor. It differs from an employment agency in that the workers are employees of the agency rather than the client. The agency "rents" them out for a fee.

PROFIT FROM THE WORK OF OTHERS

Your role is purely administrative. Rarely, if ever, do you go out on assignment yourself (unless you choose to). What you do, in effect, is maintain a list of eligible workers and assign them, as needed, to perform work for the individuals or firms engaging the services of your agency. Every hour worked by one of your employees puts a profit in your pocket.

In most categories, the surcharge is 33⅓ %. This means that if you pay an employee $2 per hour, the client pays *you* $2.65. There are, of course, some administrative expenses such as advertising and phones, and these come out of the surcharge. But the one-third add-on has been proven to be sufficient to allow for a profitable operation.

Since the workers are *your* employees, it will be your job to deduct their income taxes, Social Security, etc. This comes from, and is

based on, *the amount you pay them* (the $2 per hour in the hypo-
thetical case above) not the amount charged the client.

CONTINUE PROFITING INDEFINITELY

What is the advantage of having the workers remain *your* employees rather than the client's? Primarily, it's the fact that you continue
to profit from a man's work as long as he works. In an orthodox
employment agency, you merely collect a one-time fee, and then you
stop earning money from that man. If the man's salary were, say,
$150, and the employment agency's fee were one week's salary, $150
is the most the agency could make from that man. But if, as a
specialized help agency, you were to find the same man 40 hours of
work each week, you'd collect $2500 per year in gross profit for his
labors!

Why are clients willing to pay the one-third add-on? There are
several reasons. First, they frequently don't know how to obtain the
services of a specialist on such short notice and *must* turn to an
agency. Next, they are spared the bother of listing him as an employee and having to arrange for the deductions. Thirdly, they have
no obligation to the employee; the job is usually temporary or
sporadic, and can be terminated at any time without ill feelings.

Why are employees willing to work under such an arrangement?
Most employees of specialized agencies are persons who choose not
to be obligated to work full time. They may work a limited number of
hours per week, or they might work full time for several weeks and
then take a week or two off. It gives them much more freedom than
they would have with a regular job.

HOW TO SELECT A WINNING CATEGORY

Sixteen specialties are outlined in this chapter. After reading about
all of them, study your community and try to ascertain which services
would have the heaviest call. *Need,* after all, will be your top priority
in making a choice.

Knowledge and ability in the specialized field is also important,
although not absolutely necessary. This will make you better able to
recognize qualified job applicants and, should the need arise, fill in
during emergencies.

HOW TO BUILD A VALUABLE CLIENT LIST

Over and above the usual advertising procedures for business services of any nature—the classifieds in the phone book and the paper—there are several other client-building steps you can take.

Letters can be sent to every firm or family in your area that might have need for the category in which you specialize. Desk calendars are particularly helpful, too, since they'll be a constant reminder of your service. You can also *answer* ads for part-time help.

Once you sign up a client, do all in your power to keep him. Use special care in the selection of your employees to be sure that excellent service is provided. Insist that they report to work promptly. In the rare cases where a client and an employee don't click due to a personality clash, send a replacement cheerfully. Keep a record of your clients, and every once in a while get in touch with the inactive ones to let them know that you would like to serve them again.

Plan 1: OFFICE HELP

Many firms have need for temporary office workers to fill in during vacations, substitute for ill employees, and supplement the work force during peak periods. Stenographers and clerk-typists are the two most commonly called-upon categories, although the list also includes bookkeepers, receptionists, data processing machine operators, switchboard operators, and addressing and duplicating machine operators.

The field is so lucrative that a number of franchise firms have syndicated it, charging the franchisee a tidy sum for the use of their names and techniques. While such franchises are worth considering if you can afford them, lack of a sizable amount of capital need not hold you back. You can start an office help agency for as little as a few hundred dollars.

BUILD A "STABLE" OF EMPLOYEES

In the temporary help field, people are your inventory. Their services are all you have to sell. Your first task, then, will be to obtain a list of persons seeking to work on such a basis. Until you are well established, it's best to fill your "stable" only with people who are satisfied with working part-time. Part of your understanding with them will be that there is no guarantee of any specific number of hours to be worked per week.

Later, when you are more familiar with the needs in your area, you can begin to enroll full-time workers who will be given assignments every day. The advantage in this is their greater dependability; they rely on you for a regular salary, whereas part-time workers frequently do not.

Most of your employees will come to you through "Help Wanted" ads in the newspaper's classified section. A typical ad might go like this:

> OFFICE HELP
> Stenos, typists, bookkeepers, equipment operators, receptionists, filing clerks— work on temporary assignment to various firms, part and full time.
> ABC Temporary Help Service

TWO SOURCES OF SALARY INFORMATION

You will have to determine the going wage scales in your area for the various categories of work. Check the classifieds—they'll provide a good indication. You can also consult the nearest office of the State Employment Service for advice (and perhaps some referrals of potential employees and potential clients as well).

Remember, your employee receives whatever is determined to be the usual regional wage scale. Your fee of 33⅓% is *tacked on*. (The client need not know how much the employee is receiving; he merely pays you the $3 or $4 per hour, or whatever.)

Obtain or prepare standard job application forms and have each applicant fill one out. After determining the skills of each person, file his name under the job-titles for which he qualifies. Then you'll have a handy reference when a client seeks your services.

In some cases, you may need to have your workers bonded. Consult your insurance agent for the procedures to follow.

From time to time, a client may "steal" one of your employees from you. This happens when the client is so pleased with the person's work that he makes him an attractive job offer. It's one of the facts of life in the office substitutes business, and there is little you can do about it except to be thankful that most of your workers will prefer the freedom and variety that their arrangement with you allows.

CAPITALIZE ON SEASONAL DEMAND

In addition to the client-attracting techniques outlined earlier in this chapter, you can employ specialized tactics to reach industries in which there is seasonal demand. For example, you should contact accountants at income tax time, department stores during the Christmas season (their need for additional help is not confined to the sales force), and political committees and candidates prior to Election Day.

If you thumb through the Yellow Pages, the various listings will give you an indication of the seasonally-oriented firms in your area. Make a note to contact them at the proper time.

HOW MUCH CAN YOU EARN?

Your earnings depend, of course, on how much work you can dig up for your employees. A rule of thumb is that expenses and overhead will account for about one-half of your fee. This leaves the other half as your net profit.

Even a minimum-sized agency, in which your total billing is $25,000 per year, can earn you in excess of $3,000 for your spare-time efforts.

Plan 2: HOME MAINTENANCE, ODD JOBS

Two factors make the operation of an odd job agency particularly attractive. One is the demand for this type of work. Homeowners are constantly seeking help in maintenance chores, and most have difficulty locating people willing to provide it. Thus the services of odd job agencies are extremely welcome.

The second factor is the available labor pool. While individual homeowners may have difficulty hiring people for occasional small jobs of only a few hours duration, *you* will be able to draw from a large list of willing workers. Why? Because you'll be providing each man with a lot of work—as much as he wishes. He finds, through you, a steady source of income.

From where is your labor force drawn? From the ranks of college students, high school youngsters, retired persons, and moonlighters.

Wage scales will be based on local conditions, and on the type of work performed. And don't forget that your 33⅓% fee is added on to this scale. Homeowners hard pressed for odd job help are more than willing to pay it.

HOW ONE MAN DID IT

When the twin sons of Allen Brooks were home from college one summer, they embarked on a home-service venture that paid them well for the months of July and August. Their service consisted of window washing, floor waxing, wall washing, incidental painting, etc.

When at summer's end the twins returned to school, Mr. Brooks noted that the calls from homeowners continued to come in. People who had hired the boys and had been satisfied with their work wanted them back.

This gave Mr. Brooks an idea. Why not continue the service on a year-round basis? This does not mean that he had any thought of handling the jobs himself. In addition to having a more-than-satisfactory position with an insurance company, he had a less-than-satisfactory inclination toward any kind of manual labor.

What he did have in mind was using other people's labor.

He inserted two classified ads in the paper:

> Window washing, floor waxing, yard cleaning, other home maintenance tasks performed by Brooks Home Service Co. Call 000-0000.

> Wanted: Men and older teenagers to do home maintenance work on hourly basis. Must have car. Call 000-0000.

Mr. Brooks worked out a system in which each day he telephoned the workers on his list and informed them of their job assignments for the day. Each was supplied with a set of billheads to be filled out by the worker upon completion of the job. It was presented to the home-owner immediately, and the money paid directly to the worker. A carbon copy of each bill was retained by the worker to be turned over to Brooks along with the full payment. The worker was given his share at the end of the week.

Later, when some of the customers became "steadies" requiring work done on a regular basis, a monthly billing system was established, and the workers in these cases did not make direct collections.

HOW TO GET STARTED

The most important requirement is that you know your workers well. Interview each prospective new employee personally in order to be assured of his honesty, character, appearance, and dependability. Seek references—and check them out. Remember that the workers will be entering private homes as your representatives. Any pilfering, damage, or other transgressions can be blamed on you. Because of this, it would be wise to look into bonding your employees.

Establish card files on each worker and each customer. The cards would contain pertinent information that will assist you in matching the worker to the customer.

It is advisable to have more workers in your file than you antici-pate using. This way, when one is unavailable for duty, another can be called upon. You will then also be able to handle periods of unusually heavy workloads.

BENEFIT FROM THIS EXTRA SOURCE OF INCOME

On occasion you will be asked by your customers to perform ser-vices for which you are not prepared or equipped. You may receive inquiries concerning such tasks as painting entire homes, wallpaper-ing, furniture and rug shampooing, major repairs, installation of new siding, plastering, etc.

To meet such eventualities, it would be wise to have a list of contractors or service firms in each field—firms that will give you a commission on all jobs you obtain for them. Then, when a customer requests a particular service, you'll be able to oblige him by calling in the appropriate firm, thereby holding on to your customer and at the same time obtaining a welcome commission.

Plan 3: DOMESTIC HELP

Domestic help agencies match odd job agencies for outstanding profit potential—and for the same basic reason. It is just as difficult for people to obtain domestic help as odd jobbers.

Thus, the agency that can provide them with such help—either on a regular basis or for special occasions—will have no difficulty in attaining success.

What type of services are provided by those who work for domestic help agencies? Here's a rundown of the most commonly-performed tasks:

General household cleaning
Cook and maid service for parties
Maid service for motels and hotels during peak periods
Home care for the elderly or infirm
Substituting for housekeepers, maids, cooks, and children's nurses

Many domestic help agencies offer their customers a contract plan in which, for an established fee, homes are thoroughly cleaned on a weekly, bi-weekly, or monthly basis. The management obtains from the customer the list of required duties, and, if necessary, examines the premises before quoting the fee. The charge reflects a savings from the normal one-time fee—in effect, a "quantity discount."

In its classified advertising, one such company notes that it is able to perform "over 265 cleaning operations."

HOW TO OBTAIN WORKERS

You may have to use some salesmanship to recruit your cadre of domestic helpers. Fewer and fewer women are willing to hire themselves out for menial tasks, and your classified advertising will have to play up the advantages of obtaining part-time work that matches the spare-time hours they have available.

That is, indeed, one of the attractions of working for a domestic help agency. Because of the varied requests from customers, you'll have widely divergent work assignments and should thus be able to match the time-and-location preferences of most women you sign up.

Your recruiting may have to go beyond the classified columns. If there is a college in your vicinity, get in touch with its administrative people and ask them to pass the word concerning your agency to students seeking spare-time work. You'll be able to hire members of both sexes—with men assigned some of the heavier cleaning tasks that women often shun.

And don't neglect to contact the local office of the State Employment Service. Many people seeking part-time employment are on file there.

For the reasons explained earlier, obtaining your customers will be a breeze. Just let the word get out that you have domestic workers *willing to work,* and your phone won't stop ringing!

In fact, many domestic help agencies have waiting lists. Some customers must wait three weeks, a month, or even more before they can be serviced. Normally, this would not be a good business procedure, but when the demand outweighs the amount of available help, there is no alternative.

I have in mind a firm in the Southwest. It has some 50 workers in its active files, and each employee is working at his or her stated capacity. But still there is a waiting list. It caused the owner of the agency to raise the hourly fee from $3.75 to $4.50. Think of it— $4.50 per hour for domestic help! But, it's paid, and the waiting list has diminished only slightly.

HOW TO HOLD ONTO YOUR WORKERS

One thing to be alert for is the possibility of your workers taking customers away from you. When a woman sees you consistently receiving a sizable slice of the amount paid for her work, she may be tempted to continue working for a customer without informing you of it.

Explain to the workers that you are providing them with a service by finding the various job assignments for them. When one customer no longer needs them, you are ready with new assignments. Also explain that any employee caught moonlighting with your customers will be scratched from your list. One way to determine whether or not moonlighting is going on is to make occasional check-up calls to customers who haven't been in touch with you for a period of several months.

As your business grows and you are assured of a certain amount of activity each week, you may want to hire full-time employees instead of depending entirely on part-time workers. Eventually, one of your more dependable employees can be enlisted to help you arrange an expansion program by managing a branch in another community. One firm has established branches in five towns, and is planning on even more.

Plan 4: BABY-SITTERS

Every community needs at least one baby-sitting service, and depending on size, perhaps several. Granted, many families have among their acquaintances people who will sit for them—and generally for less money than a service would charge. But such sitters are not always available and there are a lot of families who have *not* been able to locate sitters among their friends.

Parents need a place where they can call and, even on short notice, be assured of obtaining a sitter. Most are willing to pay the additional cost.

For these reasons, a baby-sitting service administered from your home can be a highly rewarding enterprise. Naturally, the degree of financial success depends on how many sitters you can sign up and how busy you can keep them; these are some of the factors that will be considered here.

HOW TO OBTAIN SITTERS

You'll want at least 50 sitters in your active file, and preferably more. The likeliest candidates are teenagers of both sexes and older women.

Most of your employees can be located through an ad in the "Help Wanted" column. You should also contact area high schools, the State Employment Service, senior citizens clubs, and various youth organizations. And be sure to ask those who already have been signed up to refer their friends to you. Explain there won't be competition for work—there'll be enough for all.

Particular care should be taken in the selection of your sitters. This, as you know, is a responsible job. Require references from all applicants, and interview each person carefully.

The hourly wage charged by baby-sitters varies so widely from area to area that it would be useless to make any suggestions here. What you'll have to do is determine the average wage in your area, and then add on the 33⅓ % to arrive at the hourly rate your service will charge.

LET THE WORLD KNOW YOU'RE IN BUSINESS

Where is the logical place to look when you're searching for a baby-sitting service? In the Yellow Pages, of course, and this is where you should be. The ad doesn't have to be large—as long as it's there.

Many newspapers also have in their classified columns listings of various services available to area residents, and this is worth trying.

One enterprising firm made a deal with the local diaper laundry. For a small fee, the laundry agreed to insert in each batch of fresh diapers a flyer advertising the baby-sitter service.

WHAT IS THE EARNINGS POTENTIAL?

For the sake of this discussion, let us assume that the average baby-sitting rate in your community is $1 per hour. This means that your service will be charging $1.35 per hour. Your sitters must be guaranteed four hours at each job; if the parents return in less time, they still must pay for four hours.

Thus, you'll receive $1.40 as your share of the average job. If you can keep just 15 sitters busy each night, you'll be taking in $21 per night. Subtract your advertising and overhead expenses from this, and you'll probably average more than $100 per week.

TWO COLLECTION METHODS

There are two basic methods of collecting your fees. Some baby-sitting services arrange to have the fee collected by the individual sitters. Others send out bills to the customer.

There are advantages and disadvantages to each. When the sitter collects the money, he somehow has to make personal contact with you in order to transfer it. One company handles this by having the owner make a weekly round of sitters' homes to pick up their collections and pay them their shares of what has been taken in.

Billing customers is more efficient, but it sometimes means that you run into a collection problem. Families willingly pay the sitter at the conclusion of the job, but some heads-of-household put off paying bills they've received in the mail, especially when the bills are not for vital services that could be cut off for non-payment.

A firm in Wisconsin that uses the billing system finds that about 5% of its bills are not paid. But this is written off in the knowledge that it would cost more than the equivalent amount to administer a system in which the sitters handle the collections.

Plan 5: TALENT BUREAU

Entertainers are always in demand in and around your community for parties, dances, variety shows, restaurants, night clubs, and country clubs. Finding the right entertainers is often difficult, especially for those who have only occasional need for such talent.

That's why your community would undoubtedly welcome a talent bureau—a company that can provide entertainers upon request. As the operator of such an agency, you'll be dealing with singers, vocal groups, pianists, organists, combos, small orchestras, comedians, hypnotists, magicians, ventriloquists—entertainers of all types.

As with all of the other agencies outlined in this chapter, the workers (in this case the entertainers) will be employed by you rather than the customer. This is unlike the system followed by most talent agencies, which function on a commission basis.

YOUR RATE WILL BE HIGHER

You will want to receive more than the usual 10% charged by most agents. You'll be working mostly with local entertainers who have not established wide reputations, and who thus are unable to demand outstanding fees. That's why your price schedule will probably have you add 20% on to a performer's fee in the case of single acts, and a lesser percentage for acts involving more than one person (the theory being that it takes no more work to book a pair or a combo than a single).

A talent bureau serving several communities in New Jersey was launched a few years ago by a man who had never had any experience in the field, but who recognized the need. Tom Hanlon signed up his initial performers by inserting a series of small display ads in a local daily newspaper and several weeklies. Here's how one of them read:

Are You An
ENTERTAINER
Who can perform profes-
sionally? We have openings
for singers, musical groups,
comics, pianists, organists,
etc.
Talent Bureau
000-0000

Hanlon had about 20 acts on his roster within a month. Then he began a series of display and classified ads seeking bookings. In addition, he sent mailing pieces to area nightspots, and in some cases followed these up with phone calls or even personal visits.

His advertising played up the wide variety in the types of entertainment his bureau could offer. He pointed out that his firm was, in effect, "the" clearing house for local entertainment.

Hanlon's initial bookings came from several of the smaller nightclubs which required music on weekend nights. There followed a series of private parties at which music was provided, and some talent shows that he staged in their entirety as fund-raisers for local organizations (the performers cut their fees, and Hanlon cut the percentage of his add-on).

SIX TIPS FOR SUCCESS

Tom Hanlon's enterprise is typical of many similarly successful talent bureaus in various parts of the country. Here are some tips that Hanlon believes will be helpful to newcomers to the field:

• Encourage your entertainers to set their fees on the low side. Too many people get inflated ideas after reading about the tremendous money made by famous stars. When fees are reasonably low, more jobs will be available for the entertainer—and more money for you.

• When a singer or group is signed up for a long period of time at one location, it is usually best to split your part of the fee with the performer; otherwise he may be tempted to break off relations with your bureau and work out a deal with the customer. Increasing the performer's share of the fee can keep him on your list; the continuing income from a booking you obtained long ago is like found money.

• Don't overlook private parties. Individuals and organizations are often in need of music or entertainment for such occasions—ranging from children's birthday parties to large society galas.

• Be consistently on the lookout for additional performers to add to your list; the more variety you can offer, the more bookings you'll receive. Hanlon occasionally "tours" the roadhouses and nightspots in his area. When he sees a singer, musician, or group that he likes, he encourages them to consider working with his bureau.

• In most cases it will be wise not to sign up entertainers on an exclusive basis. They'll still be able to accept jobs on their own, and this fact can be helpful in convincing them to work with your bureau as well. And since you are looking for a variety of acts, chances are you'll have more performers on your list than you can provide work for on a regular basis.

• Collect the money from your customers as soon as possible after the event, while it's still fresh in their minds. Otherwise you may have difficulty collecting at all. In the case of continuous bookings at restaurants or clubs you can, of course, bill on a monthly basis.

11 MORE AGENCY PROJECTS

Office Cleaning. With the large number of people looking for part-time jobs at night, you should have no difficulty in assembling workers for night-time office cleaning. One such home-operated agency has six crews working simultaneously, and the owner netted more than $10,000 last year.

Window Washing. Believe it or not, there's a certain skill required for window washing—and a certain temperament, too. Not everyone likes climbing ladders and leaning over sills from considerable heights. Recruit a number of men who have the skill and temperament, advertise your service, and you're in business. Because of an almost universal shortage of window washing services, you'll probably get all the jobs you can handle.

Chauffeurs. You might be surprised at the number of people who, on various occasions, have need either for a car with chauffeur, or just a chauffeur. You can start a service by providing only the personnel, and then expand by buying one or more limousines. Some of your customers may be business firms, funeral homes, wedding parties, hotels, and well-to-do individuals.

Waiters, Bartenders. Business gatherings, society affairs, private parties, fund-raising events—there's a need at many of these occasions for specially-hired waiters and bartenders. Most people planning such events don't know where to turn to hire this kind of help—unless there's a waiters and bartenders bureau handy. That's where you come in.

Escorts. Particularly in large cities, escort services continue to flourish. Line up at least 20 men of good appearance and character, and insert small ads in the paper. Single women who need an escort for a special occasion, or who are visiting the city and wish to be ushered about, will comprise most of your clientele. A night out with an escort generally costs the client $20-$25 plus all expenses. You get to keep one-third of the basic charge.

Night Watchmen. You can establish a night watchman service with very little investment in money or time. Obtain a list of men (usually from the ranks of the retired) willing to work nights, and then seek out factories, warehouses, stores, and other commercial locations as your clients. You may wish to have your employees bonded.

Laborers. When a company receives a large shipment of something or other and needs it unloaded and stacked, where does it look for the needed personnel? When a firm has a sudden extra workload that requires additional men for a few days, where does it turn? In both cases, to a temporary help agency that specializes in laborers. If you live in an area where there are numerous industrial locations, this could be your spare-time business.

Visitation Service. Many elderly persons who live alone welcome the service in which, for a fee, they are "looked in on" once daily. The visitors provide brief periods of companionship, check to see that everything is all right, and even handle minor chores and errands.

Most agencies hire the *younger* senior citizens—the recently-retired—for this type of assignment.

At-Home Car Polishing. Good money is being made in a number of communities by firms that do car polishing at the customer's home. This saves the customer the time and trouble of having to transport it, and saves the firm from having to handle pick-ups and deliveries. You handle all the details from your home over the telephone—receiving the assignments and passing them on to the appropriate employees.

Sales Agency. Door-to-door selling is still a thriving industry. Many enterprising people have established their own sales agencies by obtaining exclusive rights, in their territory, to a specialized product and then signing up salesmen to peddle it. In this type of arrangement, the salesman gets the bulk of the commission (perhaps three-quarters), but your share is multiplied by the number of salesmen you have working for you. The potential can be staggering

Tutoring. Many school teachers and former teachers would like to tutor youngsters after school hours, but don't want to go to the bother and expense of advertising. You can handle this for them by establishing a tutoring service that covers all subjects taught in school. Arrange to have teachers in each subject available as needed, and then as your students are signed up, match the youngsters with the appropriate instructors. The actual tutelage can be conducted at either the student's or the tutor's home, in accordance with whichever arrangement works out best for the two individuals involved.

12

Typewriter/Camera Projects That Demand Top Dollars

Two worthy tools for use in home money-making projects are the typewriter and the camera. Their value, of course, lies in the fact that they are implements of creativity; it's not what they can do for you that makes the money, but rather what you can do with them.

The purpose of this chapter is to outline a number of the most profitable uses to which you *can* put your typewriter or camera. You'll learn the techniques that have made good money for others.

CREATE YOUR WAY TO A BANKROLL

All of the projects outlined here are creative, some more than others—but all are well within the range of the person handy with words or shutters, or both.

Because the projects *are* creative, the potential is generally greater. In a number of the plans, there is no established price for the work you are selling. It pays according to the market, and your ability to satisfy a top-paying market can upgrade your earnings potential considerably.

LITTLE-KNOWN MARKETS FOR WHAT YOU DO

A principal advantage of many of the plans contained here is that you'll find little if any competition. When most people think of earning money by writing, they think of (a) short stories, (b) magazine articles, or (c) novels. And when it comes to making money with a camera, they think of selling pictures to magazines and calendar companies.

The profit projects you'll be reading about here are those that most people *don't* think of. There's less glamor than in being a best-selling novelist or famous photographer, but there's far greater chance of achieving immediate—and consistent—success.

THREE RULES THAT GUARANTEE SALES

Obviously, the only writers and photographers who regularly make good money from their output are those who have found and have satisfied an audience. Too many who are *not* successful create for the sake of creating—for their own enjoyment, in other words—and ignore the desires of the public. Rule Number One: Tell what your audience wants and needs to know.

It frequently pays to have your material stylized so that those who see it will immediately recognize its creator. This is done not to satisfy your ego, but to develop a market by increasing the knowledge of and interest in your work. Rule Number Two: Win instant recognition with a personalized style.

The trouble with many people who launch camera or typewriter projects is that they overdo the creative bit—to the point of being cute. Don't fall into that trap. Be yourself. Report, on paper or film, clearly and concisely. Rule Number Three: Avoid undue embellishment.

Plan 1: GROUP PHOTOGRAPHY

Rare is the amateur photographer who hasn't at one time or other mused at how nice it would be if he could make his hobby pay. But most communities abound in commercial photographers who, with all of their equipment and training, have trouble making ends meet.

Thanks to this plan, you don't need their deluxe cameras and extensive background. All you need is a good reflex camera and some darkroom equipment. I know, because I've seen several people work it successfully.

One of them is Ken Burton, a man with two hobbies, one of which is photography. The other is amateur theatrics. Several years ago he was active in a thespian group that staged about four plays each year. One day the publicity director, who knew of Ken's interest in photography, asked if he could do some publicity shots in connection with a forthcoming production. The pictures would be sent to local newspapers.

Ken agreed. He decided to base his pictures on a central theme: Since the production was to be a murder mystery with an intriguing cast of characters, why not do character shots of the various performers?

He attended a Saturday rehearsal and obtained several candid pictures of each actor. That night he developed the film and printed some proofs. At the next afternoon's rehearsal, he displayed the proofs to the cast members so that each could decide which personal shot would be distributed to the papers.

Naturally, the cast members showed great interest in the shots. He was surprised that some wanted enlargements to keep for themselves.

Figuring that he could do an 8x10 for less than a dollar, including paper, chemicals, and time in the darkroom, he established a price of $3.50, and found nine customers who ordered a total of 12 pictures. The cost to him was about $8, and he took in $42.

A BUSINESS IS LAUNCHED

Ken decided right then that he would continue to do publicity work for the theatre group free of charge. And he volunteered to serve in a similar capacity for several other community organizations, including a bowling league, a volunteer fire company, and an amateur baseball team. Making sure that he snapped plenty of shots of the individual members in his publicity work, Ken found that a good percentage of them ordered prints.

A number of organizations also wanted group shots of the entire membership, and these, too, sold well on an individual basis.

The secret of Ken Burton's success is the fact that he is providing free pictures for community organizations. This is something "commercial" photographers usually won't do. So, Ken gets the assignments—and the profits from individual sales.

HOW TO BEGIN

Your first step will, of course, be to review your equipment. A good reflex camera can be obtained for a little over $100, and an excellent used one for less. Darkroom equipment need set you back no more than $200 if you stick to just what you need and skip the superfluous gadgets for the time being.

The darkroom can be portable in nature, ready to be set up in bathroom or kitchen as the need arises, or it can be permanently installed in a closet or second bathroom.

Next, you'll want to let the word get out that you are prepared to do free work for non-profit organizations. This would include publicity shots, group photos, pictures for the club bulletin—anything that involves a fairly large number of persons.

Make it clear from the outset that you will provide the organization with a specific number of prints, and that you will offer to sell additional copies to its members. Explain that this is how you are repaid for your free work—and you'll meet with few complaints.

Except for the possible printing of some business cards, you'll find advertising expense a nonentity. As soon as organization officers hear of your willingness to do free photographic work, you'll be hearing from them.

TRY SOME EXPANSION STEPS

As your reputation as a photographer becomes established, you may want to step out into other forms of work, including portraiture, commercial photography for industrial firms, etc. In fact, the chances are that you'll receive offers for these kinds of jobs, to be performed on a regular fee basis, almost from the outset.

In other words, your work for organizations can serve as the basis for your business as well as a means of getting you known and in demand for lucrative side jobs. Due to your exposure to the large numbers of people in the organizations with which you work, you will have gained a reputation without major investment for advertising or a downtown studio.

Continuing with your low overhead, you'll be able to undersell your competitors and still enjoy a larger profit margin.

Plan 2: LOCAL NEWS CORRESPONDENT

News reporting is a fascinating profession that you can enter profitably in your spare time, working from home. As a former newspaper editor and one who is currently active in broadcast news, I've seen—and in many cases hired—scores of part-time reporters. Few had any journalistic training, but all who had the time and inclination did remarkably well financially.

Is being a news correspondent a "business"? I would say so, because in practically all cases you are paid on a piecework basis for what you turn in; you are not on anybody's payroll. You are in the business of obtaining, and then selling, news and features.

Can "anybody" do it? Having the ability to write concisely and interestingly helps, but even if you can't there are still openings for you. Some stringers never write a word, phoning in their stories to rewrite men who put the material in finished form.

WHERE TO FIND ASSIGNMENTS

Your "customers" will be newspapers, radio stations, and wire services.

Newspapers. Part-time correspondents, feature writers, and reporters to cover municipal meetings are always needed by the smaller newspapers which often cannot afford the kind of full-time staff it would take to handle all of these chores, especially in outlying areas.

Typical is the story of Lola Buxton, a New Englander who several years ago contacted the editor of a paper in a city about 30 miles from where she lived—a paper that was trying to build up circulation in her community. She offered to write a twice-weekly personal news column on the doings of people in her town.

The editor quickly accepted her offer, and he promised payment of

$10 per column. But this was just the start. Not long after, the editor telephoned Mrs. Buxton and asked if she would be able to cover that night's school board meeting. This, too, would pay $10, and she could phone in her story. Mrs. Buxton agreed.

She now attends an average of two meetings per week, writes the two columns, and earns $40. She recently made arrangements with a second newspaper (in another community) to do some work for it as well, and her income is on the upswing again.

Radio and Television Stations. Broadcast stations generally do not have a news staff large enough to provide thorough coverage of the entire area in which they can be heard. Many stations that feature local news must depend upon correspondents (called "stringers" in the trade) to round out their coverage. Most often the stringers write out their own stories and read them into the telephone as an engineer or newsman at the radio station records them on a "beeper line." This is then played on the air during the course of one or more newscasts.

Some stations, however, prefer to use their stringers mainly for information which is then rewritten in the newsroom and read on the air by a regular staff member. This is particularly true of television outlets.

For example, three of the four radio stations in Westchester County, N.Y., regularly accept stories from a woman who covers civic and governmental events in the communities of Ossining and Briarcliff Manor. One of the stations uses her beepers regularly; the second occasionally uses a beeper but more often copies down the story for an announcer to read, and the third merely takes note of the information and has a staff member do a rewrite.

Wire Services. Perhaps one of the two major wire services, Associated Press and United Press International, lacks a correspondent in your area. They usually prefer to take news stories from papers or stations that subscribe to their service, but occasionally they'll agree to take important stories from people in areas where they are not represented. In most cases, all they seek is *information;* someone on the bureau desk at the wire service writes the actual story. The wire services are interested in news that has at least a regional interest, rather than material that is purely local. Included would be fatal accidents, murders, armed robberies, municipal elections and referenda, etc.

Drop a letter to the Bureau Chief in care of the nearest wire service and offer your help.

NEWSFEATURES ARE ALSO IN DEMAND

Newspapers are always looking for features. In demand are interviews with important or colorful personalities, reports on historic or interesting places, inquiring photographer columns, sports coverage, tours of government or industrial facilities, etc.

The average small newspaper keeps its full-time staffers hopping with so-called "hard news," and there may be little time left for the type of miscellany mentioned above. Editors often welcome submissions from non-staff members who are able to come up with features that are unique and interestingly presented. And you may find that once an editor has used some of your unsolicited work he'll begin giving you specific assignments that his own people are not available to cover.

Some features require the use of a camera, and, indeed, this can significantly increase the income received from your spare-time reporting.

Being handy with a camera will also allow you to earn money when you come upon such "spot news" events as accidents, fires, and protest demonstrations. You'll obtain some of these by having the foresight to carry the camera in your car wherever you go; you can also monitor police and fire radio bands for prompt word on events that might warrant photo coverage.

Plan 3: CLASSIFIED AD PAPER

One of the most popular sections in any newspaper is that which contains the classifieds. People are always interested in bargains, and that's where they can find them.

No wonder, then, that publications based entirely on classified ads have met with unusual success in many communities. Their popu-larity with readers is due to the fact that they generally contain more ads per issue, than does an orthodox newspaper. People with items to sell like them because it costs nothing to place an ad unless and until the item is sold. Payment is on a commission basis.

These publications are generally issued on either a bi-weekly or monthly basis. Because they are inexpensively produced, it is possible to launch one at home with only a modest investment. One man who started a classified ad paper as a spare-time venture several years ago has now given up his regular job and is a full-time publisher. His income averages $225 per week.

HOW TO GET STARTED

Your first decision will be to determine how large an area you wish your publication to cover. If you live in a large city, choose one section of the city. If you live in a smaller community, the entire community can be included, or you might want to cover several such towns. As a rough guideline, you might choose to serve an area of about 15,000 population to start.

After your first issue or two, there will be no difficulty in obtaining ads. But in order to meet with prompt success, your publication should contain a well-rounded selection of classifieds from the very first issue.

One way to do this is to call all of the advertisers in the classified sections of the local papers and offer to run their ads in your publication on a commission basis, explaining that they pay you only if the items are sold through the ad in your publication. Most will take you up on the offer.

You might, if you are still lacking a sufficient number, go ahead and copy all of the ads in the local papers whether or not the advertisers have agreed to the commission basis. Naturally, you won't be able to expect remuneration, but that's not the idea at this point—you're merely trying to fill out the first issues of your publication. These "borrowed" ads can be dropped as the bona fide ones increase in number.

Prominently displayed in each edition should be an invitation for readers to phone or mail in ads to you. Make this easy for them by including a coupon with your name and address. This section will also contain full information concerning the commission plan.

Most publications follow this commission schedule:

General Merchandise (Household items, tools, etc.) 10%
Motor Vehicles (Cars, trucks, motorcycles, boats,
     airplanes, etc.) 5%
Rental Property (Houses, apartments, stores) ....10% of one
                                              month's rent

The only type of advertisement for which you would be paid cash is that of a business service such as appliance repairing, fuel delivery, etc. Ads of this type would be charged on a column-inch rate that is based on the size of your circulation.

Most classified ad publications are printed by the photo offset process, which is the most practical for this type of undertaking. Initially, however, you may wish to save money and have your paper mimeographed.

In any event, you should plan to do all of the typing for the first few issues yourself. For photo offset reproduction, do it on clean white paper using a fresh black ribbon. For mimeographing, type out stencils that will be provided for you by the firm that will do the mimeographing work.

The majority of classified papers are printed on standard type-writer-sized paper (8½″ x 11″) folded once. This means that each page is actually 5½″ x 8½″. When you do your typing, you'll insert the paper or stencil sideways in your typewriter carriage. (The printer will be able to explain this to you.)

HOW TO GAIN READERSHIP

There are a number of ways in which your publication can be circulated. Every community is served by a news distributor—the company that delivers magazines and papers to the stores and stands—and your publication can be included in what he delivers.

You'll probably set an initial newstand price of about 25¢, allowing a good portion of this for the distributor and the store owner.

Other distribution methods include mailing the publication free to homes in your selected area under a bulk mailing permit, and hiring youngsters to deliver it door-to-door, along with handy subscription blanks.

It's obvious that your main income will be from the collection of commissions. While most people are honest, there are, frankly, some who will neglect to send in the money.

When an ad has appeared three or four times and you have not heard from the advertiser, give him a call. Don't disclose your identity. Say you are inquiring about the item advertised. If he says it's been sold, identify yourself and ask when you can expect the commission. If he says it has not been sold, determine if he wishes the ad to continue.

This works in most cases. Unfortunately, there will always be a few deadbeats. Of those who sell their items through your paper, it might be reasonable to expect that 15% will not pay. No matter; you'll still be making money. All classified publications consider this a routine business expense.

Plan 4: SHOPPING COLUMN

Many people are earning good spare-time incomes by conducting shopping columns in their local newspapers. These are the feature-type articles that highlight the offerings at nearby stores, reporting on sales, individual bargains, new products, closeouts, and other items of interest to consumers. This is combined with bits of chit chat and homemaking tips that hold reader interest. Store owners realize that a small mention in a news-type column is worth several times a sizable display advertisement.

Here's how the typical shopping column works: The person conducting the column purchases space in the newspaper. He or she then arranges to provide local business concerns with brief "plugs" in the column for a moderate fee. When all of the plugs are combined, the columnist receives about three times what he paid for the newspaper space. The difference between the cost of the space and the price at which it is resold to all of the retailers comprises the columnist's profit.

You may wonder why newspapers don't conduct shopping columns on their own. Although a few do, the majority would prefer to devote their attention to persuading advertisers to buy larger space units; due to high overhead and salesmen's salaries, the cost involved in selling little units is often too much for the amount of money received. The picture is different for an individual. Not having the overhead or employee problem, he can make the project financially feasible.

MEN CAN PARTICIPATE, TOO

Up until recently, most shopping columns have been conducted by women and have been aimed at a female audience. But in recent years men have been entering the field. For example, in the Southwest one newspaper carries a special column on its sports page once each week, a column that is prepared by a local sportsman and geared to fellow sportsmen. In addition to hunting and fishing news, it includes items on sportsmen's gear currently being featured at the nearby shops.

There are several columns aimed at the teenage crowd. They are financed by plugs paid for by stores catering to young people, selling such items as phonograph records, school supplies, clothing, and refreshments.

HOW TO FIGURE YOUR RATES

If the newspaper sells its space to you for two dollars per column inch and your first insertion were to be two columns wide and ten inches deep, you'd be buying a total of 20 inches and paying $40. You would then aim for $120 in sales in order to make your efforts worthwhile.

Many successful shopping columns sell their space on the basis of five-line paragraphs or units of approximately 25 words. Since the space you have purchased from the newspaper would have room for about 25 such units, your charge to the advertiser would be in the neighborhood of $5 per unit. This would give you receipts of $125.

Actually, $5 is a very modest fee for a store to pay for inclusion in a shopping column. You'll find that many stores are willing to spend much more. They can do this by buying several paragraph units at a time. For example, one columnist I know features one store each week, devoting half of her column to it. For this, the store pays $60, and management has found the expenditure fully justified by the increased sales it generates.

Getting advertisers into your first few columns will be the biggest hurdle, and even this need not be a problem if you follow a plan that has worked successfully in a number of cases.

INCLUDE FREE SAMPLES

This plan involves investing a bit of your own money. Purchase your first column and then write up tidbits on as many stores as you can include in the space. Obtain the information from their current advertising that is run elsewhere.

Then, when your column appears in print, send a copy to each of the stores mentioned. Circle the part that concerns the store to which each copy is sent, and include a brief note saying that you'll be in touch to explain how the firm can be mentioned in the column every week.

This should provide you with the basis of a fully-paid column running the following week. As it continues and becomes better known, increased sales will allow you to enlarge its size. At this point you will probably consider signing a contract with the newspaper for future advertising space—taking advantage of the lower contract rates.

Similarly, *you* can offer contract rates to those of your clients who agree to appear in your column regularly.

Sources of additional income include surcharges for firms wishing their names in bold type and for those requesting the inclusion of photographs.

Plan 5: AERIAL PHOTOGRAPHY

The camera bug who enjoys flying can combine the two pleasures and come up with a source of income that is hard to beat. Businesses, municipal agencies, newspapers, even homeowners form the market, and the prices are tops.

For example, an aerial shot can sell for $25 to $35, whereas a comparable "ground" picture would pay only $5 or $10.

And you don't have to own a plane or be a pilot to make money in aerial photography. In fact, it's better if you leave the piloting to someone else so you can concentrate on the picture-taking.

CHOOSE THE PROPER CAMERA

Most aerial photographers find that a reflex camera that uses size 120 film is the best. It's small enough so that it's not bulky or awkward to handle in the cramped cabin of a plane, and yet the image recorded on the negative is sufficiently large to allow the type of enlargement that is frequently demanded of aerial shots.

Naturally, you'll want to choose a fine-grain type of film to allow greater enlargements. The generally lower film speed on the fine-grain products will be of no concern to you, since you'll almost always be shooting in bright sunlight.

Another requirement is to have your own darkroom. It is impractical to send raw film out to a commercial processing plant and have the prints come back the way you'll need them in order to make sales. Your aerial photography will feature specific buildings and properties, and you'll want to center in on these areas when printing and enlarging. Thus, *you* have to be in the darkroom to make the key decisions.

MAKE YOUR FLYING ARRANGEMENTS

If you've got a friend who owns a light airplane, fine. You can probably work out an arrangement with him to pay for his gas and oil and have him fly you over the various spots you wish to photograph.

Otherwise, you should contact the flight service at the nearest general aviation airport and inquire about their charter rates. Explain your purpose, making it clear that the smallest, least expensive plane they have will do.

The best kind of plane for aerial photography is one in which the door on the passenger's side (the right side) can be opened, and remain open, in flight. This will provide you with a large unobstructed area for taking your photographs.

The old Piper J-3 Cubs can't be beat for photographic work. I know because I used to own one and occasionally used it to take news shots. Almost the entire side folds open, giving the largest field of view of any aircraft. In addition, they are slow enough to allow extra time for framing your shots. While this model is no longer manufactured, there are still plenty around at various airports.

HOW TO SELL YOUR WORK

Much of your work will be done on speculation, which means that you'll take the shots first and attempt to sell them later. Even if you're taking pictures on assignment, you'll want to take extra shots in the same general area "on spec," because this will lower the per-shot cost of your flight time.

A moonlighting (or, to be more precise, sunlighting) policeman of my acquaintance spends many of his free days photographing new housing developments, shopping centers, office buildings, industrial complexes, and country clubs from the air. Living in a rapidly growing area has given him no end of subjects. His pictures are all taken on speculation. He then approaches the builders or developers with the results of his work and, more times than not, makes a sale. He's found an average hour's worth of picture-taking brings in about $150.

In addition to speculative work, you might want to seek photographic assignments. Contact newspapers in your area and let them know you are available. You can also get in touch with government agencies that control parklands, recreation areas, bridges, etc. They often require aerial photographs to include in their annual reports, promotional literature, and publicity releases.

Even homeowners are potential customers. When you happen to be flying over a cluster of homes on an easily identifiable street, take shots of them (three or four houses at a time are best). Then ascertain the owners of each house and offer to sell them prints. An aerial shot of one's home is so unusual that many people jump at the chance to buy one.

16 MORE TYPEWRITER/CAMERA PROJECTS

Publicity Releases. If you have the knack of writing acceptable news copy, there's money to be made in writing news releases for business firms and organizations that want to keep before the public eye. To get an idea of how news releases are prepared, you might visit a local newspaper or radio station and ask them for a pile of old releases that they've already used. Study them for style and content, and then offer your services to prospective firms or groups.

Wedding Photography. One of the most expensive aspects of a wedding is hiring the photographer. Working out of your home, you can charge considerably less than a downtown photographer does—and still earn a good profit. Have a circular printed and send it to everyone listed in the engagement columns of the local newspapers.

"Action" Reporter. A feature that more and more newspapers are adopting is the column in which consumer complaints are resolved. Readers write in outlining the trouble they've had getting refunds, service, delivery, etc. The columnist, backed by the power of the press, straightens out the difficulties with the business involved. Then the reader's original letter is printed in the column, followed by the "action" report. Offer to do this type of column for your local newspaper. The fee paid you by the paper should be tentative, allowing you to determine from experience how long the work involved in each column takes; then a permanent fee can be set.

Movie Documentaries. With the arrival of 8mm sound movies, a creative Massachusetts resident earned some extra spending money by producing a documentary supporting an anti-pollution drive sponsored by a service club. He was paid $350 for the film, which was so well received that two other groups have since asked him to produce documentaries for them.

Syndicated Editorials. Weekly newspapers and small radio stations frequently welcome the submission of editorials for them to consider printing or broadcasting. These small firms don't always have the staff or the time to handle editorials themselves. A number of individuals make money by writing weekly editorials of general interest and then submitting them to the media. It can be done on a subscription basis (at an annual rate) or on the understanding that each paper or station pays for only those editorials it uses. Directories of papers and stations are published by Standard Rate and Data Service, and are available in many libraries.

Tavern License Photos. A New Yorker has profited from his state's requirement that new taverns, and existing ones that plan alterations, file photographs of the construction or change. Whenever he spots a new tavern being built, or alterations going on at an existing one, he contacts the proprietor and offers to take the necessary pictures. Check with the Liquor Authority in your state to determine if there are similar photographic requirements.

Trade Magazine Features. If you've a yen for seeing your prose work in print, one of the easiest and most profitable ways to do it is by submitting feature articles to trade magazines. Your raw material can come from newspaper clippings on subjects relating to the trade on which the magazine is based, or from interviews with people active in the field. Your best bet is to submit outlines first, and proceed with the actual writing after the editors give the o.k.

Beachstroller. A native of the sunny state of Florida makes good money during the tourist season by marching up and down the beaches, camera in hand and a signboard strapped to his torso. The message on the signboard is that for $1 he'll snap a picture of an individual or a couple, with the resultant print to be in the form of a postcard. Vacationers are very pleased at the prospect of having a personal card to send to the folks back home. Early each evening the beachstroller develops the day's photos and pastes each to 3¼ x 5½″ stock, imprinted with the usual postcard insignia on the back. He offers reduced rates for additional postcard copies of each photo for tourists wishing to mail out several, and the finished work is delivered to the hotel desk for pickup by the vacationers that night.

Resume Writing. A lot of people who are exceptionally qualified for the kind of job they are seeking don't, nevertheless, know how to prepare an adequate resume. You can provide this service for them, from composing the basic presentation to having it reproduced in the quantity requested by the client. Ernest A. Gray of Pound Ridge, N.Y., features such a service "for executives only" and reports outstanding success.

Passport and Chauffeurs' Photos. Applicants for passports and chauffeurs' licenses need "mug shots" to submit with their applications. If you live on a well-traveled road, hang a shingle in front of your home; otherwise advertise in the classifieds.

Club Bulletins. Armed with a typewriter and a mimeograph machine, you can edit and print the monthly club bulletins so many organizations like to issue. Numerous groups don't have members willing or equipped to handle the chore, so they welcome an opportunity to have it done commercially.

Home Listings. Many real estate brokers like to maintain files of photographs of the homes they have listed to assist the client in deciding which ones he wants to inspect. A tidy income can be earned by arranging with several brokers to take care of this photographic work for them.

Company Newspapers. An at-home worker in the Northwest has developed a full-time business out of preparing house publications for a number of companies in her area. Her clients are firms that are not large enough to be able to afford a full-time editor, but which nevertheless are willing to pay for publication of a house organ, usually on a monthly basis. The client-companies assign one employee in each department to provide the editor with appropriate news items concerning the department and its workers. These items are then edited to fit the format of the publication, and when compiled with the news of the other departments, comprise a most interesting journal of company and employee activities.

Custom Darkroom Work. Many amateur photographers are not satisfied with the automated type of developing and enlarging they get from most processing labs. That's why the photographers in your area would welcome a custom lab in which you do the work precisely to their specifications. A well-equipped darkroom is, of course, a must.

Advertising Brochures. Where does a small firm turn when it needs a professionally-produced brochure to advertise its wares? To you, hopefully. Many individuals with advertising and/or graphic arts experience specialize in this type of work. You can make arrangements with a printer to do the actual presswork, enabling you to offer a complete package, beginning with the idea and makeup and concluding with the finished brochures.

Slide Duplication. Many people own treasured 35mm slides that they would like copied. With a simple attachment to your own 35mm camera, you can make these duplicates for them. Send your exposed film to an overnight processing lab, and you can provide almost instant service.

13

A Potpourri
of Profit Plans

In the course of the past twelve chapters you have gained quite a business education. Reading all of the plans presented so far has enabled you to assimilate a wealth of knowledge that might otherwise have taken years of experience to attain.

The fact is, you can now consider yourself well-versed in the principles and techniques of conducting a successful home enterprise. You've seen these principles and techniques applied in scores of different ways in scores of different profit plans. You'll know how and where to use them when they are needed in your own business.

Because you do have this foundation of knowledge, you can absorb new business plans more rapidly. You don't need them spelled out for you step by step. And that's what makes the rapid-fire presentation in this chapter possible. You *know* the basics . . . now you're about to learn 20 new ways to apply them.

Actually, this chapter differs from its predecessors in two ways. First, the businesses are presented in a much more concise manner. Second, there's no central theme; businesses in many different categories are suggested here, each one chosen because of its proven record and ease of operation.

It's a well-rounded selection that adds more options to the already hefty list of uses to which you can put your new-found knowledge.

FLOOR WAXING SERVICE

Inlaid linoleum is more in use than ever before, and the need for commercial polishing services has increased right along with it.

Armed with a heavy-duty buffer, you can launch such a service. As your customer list grows, you can purchase additional buffers and hire people to run them. Eventually, you can "retire" from the physical end of the business and devote more of your time to administrating.

Your customers will include offices, factories, restaurants, stores, hotels, and motels. Although there's a lot of linoleum in use in private homes, the amount of it *per home* is generally too meager to be profitable.

One of the advantages of owning a floor polishing service is that you don't need to be constantly in search of new business. It's a "repeat sale" type of thing; customers pleased with your work will want you back regularly.

In fact, most polishing services work on a contract basis. Their rates are based on performing each job periodically, be it bi-weekly, weekly, or (in some large establishments with heavy traffic) more frequently.

Gain your customers initially via business card, classified ad, mailing piece, or personal visit. Once you've reached your capacity, there should be little turnover if you provide satisfactory service. You may even find yourself with a waiting list for use in replacing customers who do drop out.

LEATHERCRAFT

Leathercraft has had a comeback. Products handmade of leather are "in," selling at excellent prices over the counter and through the mail

While experience as a hobbyist in this type of craft will get you off to a faster start, you can learn the necessary skills by picking up a book or two at your library or bookstore, or by signing up for an adult ed course.

With the skills thus acquired, you'll be prepared to make and sell such items as: apparel (gloves, shirts, skirts, jackets, belts, sandals, slippers), billfolds, book covers, bookmarks, brief and attaché cases, credit card holders, desk pads, golf bags, key cases, picture frames, and purses.

You can sell your output at retail, or you can wholesale it to established dealers.

The methods of handling your own retail sales range from roadside stands on heavily-traveled thoroughfares (particularly if you live in a tourist area) to mail order. Several highly successful mail order enterprises are based entirely on leather products produced by the firms themselves.

Dealing through other retail outlets can free you to devote more time to actual production. One type of outlet to consider is that of roadside stands operated by people who sell their own non-competitive products. Department stores and gift shops in your area might also be good purchasers. In addition, church bazaars and regional arts and crafts shows can produce significant sales.

SPECIAL SERVICE LAUNDRY

Although the ease of operating automatic washers and driers means that most people do their own laundries these days, many are not willing to tackle delicate fabrics, woolen sweaters, and hard-to-clean articles. A profitable home-based business can be launched by performing these services.

Most commercial laundries are not geared to handle such items. Their profit comes from volume work, and it would be prohibitive for them to take on hand-washed material or those that require special settings on the washer.

Many women are realizing spare-time incomes by operating special service laundries that handle items ranging from angora to Zefran. They've learned the techniques from available books on the subject. One of the most complete is *How to Clean Everything* by Alma Chesnut Moore, published by Simon and Schuster in the hardcover edition and by Pocketbooks in paperback.

Handling special items in your home laundry means that you'll be able to demand a premium over what the commercial laundries charge for routine items. Because of the specialized service you're offering, your customers will happily pay the premium.

P.A. RENTALS

Stock up on several public address systems and you've got the foundation of a "sound" source of extra income. Scores of organizations in and around your community have occasional need for this type of equipment. Since these once or twice-per-year functions are not sufficient cause for these organizations to buy their own P.A. systems, they rent them.

Most auditoriums have built-in systems, so the call for your equipment will be for functions that are held out-of-doors or in buildings not normally used for mass assemblages.

Examples: Outdoor commencement exercises, scouting award ceremonies, square dances, charitable auctions and bazaars, church events at which overflow crowds are expected, political rallies, lectures, sporting events.

Your chief business-creators will be the Yellow Pages and appropriate classified listings in the local papers.

Rental fees will be based on the type of amplifier needed and the number and type of speakers. The minimum fee for a rental period of up to one day is $15, provided the items are picked up from and returned to your door. The one-day fee for more elaborate setups can range up to $50 or $75, and even more if your personal services are needed for installation and/or operation.

HOME BEAUTY SHOP

Because space requirements are relatively small, the beauty shop business lends itself very well to private homes. One large room properly outfitted is all you need.

If you have the necessary license and training for hair-styling, the odds are that you have been employed in one or more beauty shops in your area. If so, your name will be familiar to a lot of your former customers. Take advantage of this by advertising in the local newspapers and displaying your name prominently in each ad.

If you have not worked locally before, you'll have to build your reputation from scratch. Your first few satisfied customers will provide the start when they refer their friends to you. But here are a few ways to speed things up:

Volunteer your services at fashion shows in exchange for receiving credit in the printed programs and from the commentator; teach adult education classes on personal grooming; give a $100 scholarship to a deserving high school graduate interested in a career in beauty culture; write articles on hair-styling for the local papers.

BUILT-IN FURNITURE

In Plan 6 of Chapter 5 we discussed wood products created in the home workshop; this centered on choosing and manufacturing one particular product in quantity. Many craftsmen-in-wood take the other route with equal success: They perform custom work, making one-of-a-kind pieces to fit the specific needs of their customers.

Rare is the home that would not be enhanced by the addition of built-in units. Their purpose can be to help resolve a lack of storage space or to improve the appearance or functional value of a particular corner or wall.

Frequently requested built-ins include cabinets of every type for every room of the home, shelves, high fidelity enclosures, wall dividers, storage compartments, desks, window seats, door racks, bunk beds, and fold-up tables.

The major components of these items can be pre-assembled in *your* home, with the finishing touches applied upon installation in the customer's home.

You can obtain your customers through small ads, business cards, a sign on your lawn, and word of mouth. Second only to obtaining a customer is establishing a clear-cut understanding with him. *You* must know precisely what it is that he wants, and *he* must know precisely what he's going to get for his money. A built-in piece of furniture is not something you can sell to someone else if the customer for whom it was built rejects it.

In Mexico recently, I visited a woodworking shop with a plaque on the wall bearing these words: *Mi lema es — satisfacer al cliente.* Translated: "My motto is 'Satisfy the client.'" It should be your motto, too.

LAND PROJECTS

The old saying, "He couldn't see the forest for the trees," is, unfortunately, very apt. Many of us fail to recognize opportunity that is literally in our back yards.

There's money to be made in woodland and other uncultivated areas. If you own such acreage, you should be profiting from it; if not, but if there is some nearby, chances are that several sources of profit remain open to you. Some examples follow.

Food Products. Many edible foods grow wild. A housewife in Michigan's upper peninsula makes thimbleberry jam on a commercial basis in her kitchen. Her crew includes one kitchen helper and about 30 children who pick the wild thimbleberries. Much of the jam is sold to tourists, and some mail orders are filled. Other woodland food products include wild honey, walnuts, persimmons, blueberries, wild rice, mushrooms, and maple syrup.

Soil Conditioners. The production and marketing of wood, bark, and foliage of trees for use in soil treatment can provide varied sources of income and fuller use of woodland materials. A cattle farmer in the coastal plain section of the South adds to his income by baling and selling pine straw to large nurseries. Sixty bales per acre can be yielded.

Much of the material used to improve soil is mixed into croplands as they are prepared for planting. The materials include sawdust, shavings, wood chips, ground bark, and pine needles.

Wood By-Products. Many trees and shrubs contain aromatic oils, resins, or acids that can be sold to commercial firms for use in manufacturing adhesives, paints, varnishes, paper, soaps, plastics, perfumes, pharmaceuticals, insecticides, polishes, and other items.

A thriving business enterprise in southeastern Maine is based on balsam fir needles. For more than 30 years, the family that owns the business has found good profits in making incense, fireplace powder, and souvenir pillows stuffed with needles.

Plants and Brush. A man in the state of Washington has received an income from his land for several years without touching the timber. The money has come mainly from the sale of huckleberry and salal brush. Some wild plants such as rhododendron, laurel, azalea, and leucothoe are salable just as they come from the forest.

INTERIOR DECORATING

This is not a field you can pick up overnight, but provided you have a certain flair it's worth learning. There can be exceptional financial rewards in lending your expertise to others. Once the rudiments are yours (and you can practice on your own home) all you'll really have to know in order to go into business is how and where to buy the furnishings and materials you'll need to carry out your assignments.

Become familiar with the offerings in the local stores, and with those in the nearest large city. Then, through the interior decorating and women's magazines, learn what is available through the mail.

Interior decorators usually specialize in one type of assignment. The specialties include:

Homes and apartments
Model homes
Offices
Restaurants

Most decorators of homes and apartments have their own favorite styles ranging from the foreign influence (French, Italian, or Spanish) to early American or perhaps modern. The decorators build reputations on these styles and gain many clients from among those who have seen their finished work.

Decorating model homes is particularly profitable in areas where the population is rapidly growing and many new housing developments are being built. Become known by a number of real estate agents and builders and you should find yourself with plenty of work.

Decorating offices and restaurants is another specialty where doing one top-rate job can lead to several new assignments.

DIAPER SERVICE

Because you're working from home, you can undersell the competition and steal many of its customers. This works for numerous types of businesses, among them diaper services. And all you need to start are a dependable washer, drier, and car.

Later, you can add additional machines as you need them, and eventually you might convert to commercial equipment.

You'll gain your customers by offering lower prices than—but comparable service to—any other diaper laundry in the area.

Stock up on a thousand or so diapers, buy a number of covered plastic hampers (one to be loaned to each customer) and begin your advertising. Newspaper ads should be augmented with mailing pieces or phone calls to new mothers. Get their names from local hospitals or from announcements in the paper.

Most diaper services make two pickups per week, giving the customer fresh diapers equivalent in number to those that are taken in for cleaning. The fee varies according to locality; if in your area the large companies charge $16 per month, you'll probably offer the same service for $13.

HOME CLEANING EQUIPMENT RENTALS

Money can be saved when women shampoo their own rugs and overstuffed furniture, especially if they don't have to invest heavily in shampooing equipment.

Money can be *made* if you rent this equipment to them—along with floor polishers and buffers.

The way to enter the business is to work out arrangements with one or more local stores (preferably food markets or general stores) to place the rental items on display. For providing the space and handling the rentals, the store owner gets to keep 20-25% of the fee. He also benefits from the sale of shampooing materials and floor waxes that are used with the rented equipment.

You can start out with as few as three shampooers and three polishers placed in one store. Try to arrange it so that they are given prominent display along with a fairly large sign explaining the rental setup.

From the initial activity with these six machines you'll be able to judge how many more would be warranted for that same store—and how many you should attempt to place in stores in other neighborhoods.

Later, you might add floor sanding machines to your inventory.

INVESTING IN SECOND MORTGAGES

Few people—except those who have already been on the profit side of this type of endeavor—recognize the earnings that are available in second mortgages.

Purchasers of new homes or income property often require greater financing than is available to them under the first mortgage. They generally turn to second mortgages and are willing to pay the higher interest rates such loans carry.

Many experts agree that if the proper precautions are taken, second mortgaging can be a remarkably safe and conservative type of investment. But, you ask, what's it doing in a book such as this—doesn't it require a big outlay of cash?

Not if you take the word of Joseph L. Steinberg, attorney and real estate investor. He's written a book entitled *Mortgage Your Way to Wealth: The Principle of Supplemental Real Estate Financing,* published by Parker Publishing Company, Inc. In it, Mr. Steinberg says you can start with as little as $1500, and earn a whopping 56.8% accumulated return.

For a money-making endeavor that requires only minimum management attention, that kind of return is hard to beat.

CORRESPONDENCE COURSES

Did you know that most correspondence courses contain little more information than can be found in a good textbook? But while a textbook might cost six, seven, or eight dollars, the correspondence course can sell for 50 times that much!

It's estimated that there are between 500 and 1,000 privately-run home study firms in the United States, and a good many of them are conducted by individuals who are themselves operating from home.

There are two ways to get into this business. If you have exceptional knowledge in a field in which you believe a number of people would be interested, you can prepare your own course material.

Or, lacking the knowledge or inclination to prepare an entirely new course, you can supply your students with existing textbooks. Orthodox schools and colleges, after all, use textbooks as the basis of their instruction and there is no reason why you can't, too.

Correspondence courses using regular textbooks supplement them with study guides and booklets containing the quizzes that follow each assignment.

There's a difference between correspondence courses and correspondence schools. While I know of no restrictions preventing anyone from preparing and selling a *course* provided he gives honest value, there are varying state laws regarding *schools*. So don't try to pass yourself off as, say, The American School of Fundamental Bricklaying unless you really do run a bona fide school replete with a staff of instructors.

Many firms do, however, legitimately sell home study *courses* which consist of printed text material and brief quizzes. Without pretending to be full-fledged schools, institutes, or colleges, they do very well financially. This is the least complicated way for you to enter the business.

For information on how to sell your course to prospective students, re-read Chapter 4 in this book.

SHOPPING SERVICE

With the increase in the number of supermarkets and the steady decrease in the number of corner grocery stores, one formerly-available service is sorely missed: Food delivery.

The housewife used to be able to call the corner grocer, place her order, and receive the goods at her kitchen door later that day. But not now. The supermarkets work on markups that are much closer than those of their predecessors, and they can't even *think* about offering delivery service.

This can put you in a very nice position. Launch a shopping service, advertising the fact that you will do shopping at any of the major centers in your area. (It's best to avoid out-of-the-way stores, because you'll want to shop for several customers simultaneously, and time is an important profit factor.)

How much can you charge? A shopping service I know of in the South adds 10% to the price of the food purchased, with a minimum fee of $1.50. This means that his customers are paying 10% more than they would if *they* went to the stores—but they're saving on auto wear and tear as well as their own time and effort. Many women find it well worth it, and the owner of the service has found it profitable. He began with the family station wagon, but now uses a panel truck.

PUBLISH A NEWSLETTER

Magazines with 100-200 pages sell for 50¢-$1.00. Newsletters with 4–8 pages sell for up to $4 per copy! Hard to believe? It's true—and the amazing thing about it is that newsletters are extremely simple to produce. The masters are prepared on a regular typewriter and then duplicated on a photo offset press for pennies per copy.

Can *you* publish a newsletter? You can if you have specialized knowledge, or *access* to specialized knowledge in a field in which there is significant interest.

Why do people pay so much to subscribe? Because either (1) they are unable to obtain the information from any other source, or (2) they are too busy to keep up with all of the magazine and newspaper articles on the subject and require this information to be carefully distilled for them.

Newsletters are published on hundreds of subjects, but some of the most popular cover such fields as the stock market, income taxes, real estate investments, legislation, business trends, medical news, health and fitness, etc.

Newsletters are sold through the mail, so the mail order rules outlined in Chapter 4 apply.

ANSWERING EQUIPMENT RENTALS

The increasing availability of dependable machines that will answer the telephone while the subscriber is away and record the messages voiced by callers can be a boon for you.

There's money to be made in renting such equipment to businessmen. True, the machines can be purchased outright by anybody who wants one—but then he must arrange for his own maintenance after the 90-day guarantee period has expired.

Your service will include installation and maintenance. You might even have a lease-purchase plan in which the businessman can have his monthly rental (usually about $15) applied to the purchase price. This allows him to try a machine for a while and then decide if he wishes to purchase it.

The best way to get started is to have yourself appointed a dealer by a manufacturing or a distributing firm. This will probably make it necessary for you to purchase a number of machines, but you'll be needing them anyway. And you'll have the advantage of paying the wholesale rather than the retail price. In addition, you'll be able to obtain the manufacturer's service manuals to guide you in whatever maintenance you may be called on to do, and you'll be able to order parts as needed.

Since you'll be sticking with one basic brand, make your selection carefully. Don't settle on a brand until you have tried it out in your own home, preferably for a period of several days.

Do your advertising in the Yellow Pages, and circularize likely prospects *listed* in the Yellow Pages—including repair shops, accountants, attorneys, physicians, and any businessman who is likely to spend a good deal of his time away from his shop or office.

USED PIANOS

You'll need a pickup or panel truck, and you'll have to take some training in tuning and repair (home study courses are available) but you'll find that there's a big market for used pianos.

The reason for the demand is the high cost of new pianos—and the fact that used instruments can be every bit as good as those fresh out of the showroom.

Here are three of the firms offering home study courses in tuning and repair:

American School of Piano Tuning
P.O. Box 707,
Gilroy, Cal.   95020

Capital Piano Tuning School
3160 S.W. 16th Court,
Ft. Lauderdale, Fla.   33312

Niles Bryant School
3631 Stockton Boulevard,
Sacramento, Cal.   95820

Once you have the ability to tune and repair pianos, you can begin purchasing used ones through the classified ads in the paper. Repair and refinish them when necessary—and resell them via the same method—the paper. The fact that you have a means of delivering them will help speed sales.

You can also work out arrangements for periodic tuning of the pianos you've sold . . . for a fee, of course.

SALES OF REFURBISHED HOMES

Your headquarters for handling the few administrative details involved will be *your* home, but your source of profit will be the past and future homes of other people. The idea is to purchase rundown residences, spruce them up, and then sell them at a good profit.

No great expertise is required, merely a lot of spare time. The only skills you'll need are those of a handy man . . . or woman. (Women have been particularly successful at this. I know one who has averaged at least $8,000 per year in her spare time.)

Because the best buys in rundown homes are not often listed in the newspaper ads, you'll have to do some searching in order to find your "raw material." Search for places with "For Sale" signs on the lawn (or tacked to the front if the grass is typically high). Visit real estate agents and let them know what you're looking for.

Sometimes just a good coat of paint inside and out is all that's required to give you a profit of several thousand dollars. Other times, some plastering or installation of new wallboard may be required. Where the plumbing or heating systems are outmoded, you may have to call in outside help. Keep a record of all such expenditures so you can take them into account when setting your resale price for the refurbished house.

You can try selling your completed buildings yourself through signs and ads, and thus save the broker's commission. Or you can save *time* (and use it to work on your next property) by having a broker do all the showing.

PET PARADE

Nobody has ever taken a census of the number of pets that stray from home, but the figure would be astounding. Helping to return these pets can be a lucrative sideline.

Most newspapers run lost and found columns, but there's a delay of at least a day and perhaps two or three before an ad appears in print. You can provide an instant service.

How? By means of automatic telephone answering equipment that spiels off a recorded message whenever anyone calls your number. Changing the recording two or three times daily, you can list all of the lost and found animals reported to you by residents of your community.

There are two ways to be paid for this service. You can establish a basic fee of perhaps a dollar to be paid by everyone inserting a lost or found notice. The price is so low that you won't be able to send out any bills; when people phone in their ads, give them your mailing address and put them on the honor system.

The other method, and one that can bring a greater return, is to sell spoken advertisements to appropriate business firms such as pet and animal food stores. To have a "captive" audience, the advertisement is read prior to the listing of the losts and founds.

CHILDREN'S HOTEL

Many couples would like to enjoy occasional overnight or weekend trips without having the bother of caring for their children. Realizing this, a woman who lives in a town not far from Milwaukee provides a service in which the children can be deposited at her home and cared for and fed until the parents return.

She even maintains one room as an infants' nursery where babies can be left by parents who will be gone for only a few hours, but who have not been able to find a baby sitter.

Rates at the "hotel" vary according to the age of the child and the number of meals consumed. The house is well stocked with games for the older children and also has a TV set, a piano, and a phonograph. The fenced-in yard has swings, slides, and seesaws to keep the youngsters amused on pleasant days.

Small newspaper ads and the passing of the word by pleased parents keep the hostelry filled with guests.

It would be appropriate here to repeat the advice first given in Chapter 2, and that is to check with a competent insurance agent concerning coverage. When you care for children, there can be accidents and illnesses, and you'll want to be financially protected for liability. Also check local regulations to determine what, if any, license might be required.

EXERCISE EQUIPMENT

Everyone wants to be physically fit, and some people actually work at it. Sales of exercise equipment have skyrocketed. So have rentals.

Operating from your home, you can open an exercise equipment rental agency and perhaps make some sales as well. Many people hesitate to purchase equipment that they fear they may soon tire of using or may find ineffective for their particular needs. These are the people who are key rental prospects.

The types of equipment that can be leased to them include stationary bicycles, real bicycles, rowing machines, weightlifting paraphernalia, jogging treadmills, "home gyms," vibrating devices, exercise mats and boards, and sports equipment.

These items are rented on a weekly or a monthly basis, and frequently the fee can be applied to the purchase price should the customer want to keep the equipment.

You may be able to work out an arrangement with local health food stores to have your posters placed in the window or on an interior wall, and also to have one of your circulars inserted in outgoing bags of food. It might even be a "trade" deal in which you advertise each other.

*   *   *   *   *   *

When a housewife finishes mixing a cake batter, she puts it in the oven, and the batter comes to life, expanding and taking on shape. All of the ingredients were there before she put the pan in the oven, of course, but nothing could happen until the heat was applied.

That batter can be likened to the contents of this book. The ingredients of your success are here, but they can only be effective if you light the fire.

Go to it.

Index